MASTERING SUBJECT SPECIALTIES

MASTERING SUBJECT SPECIALTIES

SPECIALTIES

Practical Advice from the Field

Karen Sobel, Editor

LIBRARIES
UNLIMITED™
An Imprint of ABC-CLIO, LLC
Santa Barbara, California • Denver, Colorado

Library of Congress Cataloging-in-Publication Data

Names: Sobel, Karen, editor.
Title: Mastering subject specialties : practical advice from the field / Karen Sobel, editor.
Description: Santa Barbara, California : Libraries Unlimited, an imprint of
    ABC-CLIO, LLC, [2016] | Includes bibliographical references and index.
Identifiers: LCCN 2015043485 (print) | LCCN 2016004590 (ebook) | ISBN
    9781440839641 (pbk : acid-free paper) | ISBN 9781440839658 (ebook)
Subjects: LCSH: Academic librarians—Vocational guidance—United States. | Special
    librarians—Vocational guidance—United States. | Academic libraries—Relations
    with faculty and curriculum—United States.
Classification: LCC Z682.4.C63 M37 2016 (print) | LCC Z682.4.C63 (ebook) |
    DDC 023/.2—dc23
LC record available at http://lccn.loc.gov/2015043485

ISBN: 978–1–4408–3964–1
EISBN: 978–1–4408–3965–8

20 19 18 17 16   1 2 3 4 5

This book is also available as an eBook.

Libraries Unlimited
An Imprint of ABC-CLIO, LLC

ABC-CLIO, LLC
130 Cremona Drive, P.O. Box 1911
Santa Barbara, California 93116-1911
www.abc-clio.com

This book is printed on acid-free paper (∞)

Manufactured in the United States of America

CONTENTS

CONTENTS

PART II

INTRODUCTION

Karen Sobel
University of Colorado Denver

If you asked me what I love most about academic subject specialist librarians, I would give you two answers in no particular order. Answer A: They continually pursue their intellectual passions, explore new avenues, talk to experts in the field, seek out information through presentations and other active media, read widely, and evolve. Answer B: They are unfailingly generous people who enjoy helping others meet their research-oriented goals. Both of these factors helped to inspire *Mastering Subject Specialties: Practical Advice from the Field.*

INSPIRATION FOR THIS BOOK

When I was a library school student at the University of North Carolina at Chapel Hill, I was fortunate to have a sea of subject specialists surrounding me. My supervisors and colleagues told me to seek out specialists in the fields that interested me and to ask as many questions as I could. In some cases, these interactions led me to pursue internships and other work experiences to develop my skills in several fields. These subject specialists were uniformly generous and detailed with their guidance.

Not all of us are fortunate enough to have such a perfect setting for exploration. Some may have recently started our studies in librarianship and not yet connected with a community of experts. Others may work in libraries that do not have the entire range of expertise offered in this book. *Mastering Subject*

Specialties aims to share honest, thorough advice from subject specialists with those who may be interested in entering similar fields or simply exploring the range of possibilities. The chapter authors are predominantly established experts in their fields. Some have held high-level leadership roles in librarianship, such as Dixie A. Jones, past president of the Medical Library Association. Others are newer librarians and rising stars in their fields.

SELECTING PORTIONS TO READ

All readers should of course pursue the chapters on the subject specialty or specialties that interest them the most. It's well worth reading about specialty areas in which you have completed at least some college-level coursework. As you will learn through the chapters that follow, some specialty areas lean toward expecting a particular undergraduate or graduate degree, while others tend to develop through on-the-job training. You may learn that you are nearly qualified for a specialty you had not considered before. Or you might realize that you should pursue some additional coursework or an internship before you can realistically be considered for a position in a certain area. Either way, gathering more information can help you move forward.

Current master of library science students should also read "Factors Affecting Most Subject Specialist Positions." This chapter discusses the myriad qualities of academic institutions that have practical effects on librarians' work. For instance, a library serving 40,000 students tends to be quite different from one serving 3,000 students. A campus with a medical school tends to have different health-related resources and services than one without a medical school. Until you've worked in academic libraries, you probably can't anticipate how these factors will affect your work and life. It's helpful to learn a bit about how these factors affect jobs and workplaces before you begin applying to positions.

Experienced librarians who have an interest in changing specialties will benefit from the final two chapters, "Changing Fields within Academic and Research Libraries" and "Preparing to Move Up the Ladder." "Changing Fields within Academic Libraries" guides librarians on how to harness the experience they already have to excel at a job in a new field in an academic library. Librarians can also use ideas in this chapter to help make a case for what they would bring to a job in another field. "Preparing to Move Up the Ladder" explores different ways that academic librarians choose to move forward in their careers. It suggests actions librarians can take in order to prepare themselves to take on more responsibility and meet their career goals.

OUTLINE OF CHAPTERS

All of the chapters covering a specialty have a similar outline. I asked each of the authors to respond to these eight questions:

1. With what other subject specialties does your specialty area cross boundaries?
2. What range of libraries or other settings does this type of specialist work in?
3. Are there any special requirements for a position in your field, such as additional college degrees or languages spoken?
4. What master of library science and other coursework would help prepare a librarian for this specialty?
5. What types of internships and work experience would help prepare a master of library science student to work in this field?
6. Do librarians in this field tend to move up the "ladder" in a certain way?
7. Which professional organizations are important in your specialty area?
8. Which professional or scholarly publications provide the best information in this field?

Each of the authors made an effort to balance his or her personal judgment and experiences with standards and norms in his or her subject area. The authors carried through beautifully, writing pieces that are both thorough and personable.

PASSION

The joy the authors find in their work seeps through the connotative language they use in their chapters. In fact, biological sciences librarian Kelli Trei and I discussed the happiness that comes through in her writing. She and I had a delightful exchange in the comments section in the "Track Changes" mode of Microsoft Word in which she exclaimed, "It [science librarianship] *does* make me happy!" I hope that readers, wherever they may be in their studies, their careers, or their exploration of avenues, will find jobs that give them this much happiness as well.

DON'T HESITATE TO ASK

If you find that you have questions after reading this book—true librarians generate more questions the more they learn—consider getting in touch with a librarian in a subject specialty that interests you. If you choose to do so, try to find someone you have some sort of connection with, such as a librarian who works nearby or someone who belongs to a professional organization that you've joined. Get in touch with him or her and ask if you could meet for an hour (offer an outing to a venue with a lot of choices of tea—librarians like that), talk over the phone, or e-mail. Come up with a list of specific, focused questions to ask when you meet or talk. Most librarians enjoy talking about their profession and nurturing potential colleagues.

THANKS

Huge, heartfelt thanks to the chapter authors for their generous and thoughtful writing. You are so very talented and wonderful to work with. Thanks to Lise

Dyckman, former editor at Libraries Unlimited, for making the writing and editing process so smooth, and for helping me to find solutions to all of my tough questions. Thanks to the University of Colorado Denver for giving me sabbatical time during which I completed this book. And thanks most of all to my beloved family, Eric and Nora.

FACTORS AFFECTING MOST ACADEMIC LIBRARY SUBJECT SPECIALIST POSITIONS

Karen Sobel
University of Colorado Denver

Before you flip to the chapters detailing the subject specialties that interest you the most, spend a few minutes learning about factors that link all of the specialties. This chapter helps you understand how the institution housing a specific job shapes the work that that librarian will do. It highlights major factors to be aware of and provides ideas on how to find out more at an individual institution. While the list of factors here is by no means comprehensive, investigating these topics will help a new librarian predict how the setting and requirements of a potential job might shape his or her life.

Characteristics of both a specific library position and the academic institution where it's located will affect a librarian dramatically. When an individual is new to the job market, though, figuring out which factors to research in order to predict a little bit about what the job will be like can prove challenging.

ABOUT THE POSITION AND THE LIBRARY

Tenure and Research Requirements

Many of the chapter authors originally mentioned tenure and research requirements in their chapters. Since these topics can affect any position in academic libraries, I chose to discuss them in this broader chapter—but you can see that they are on the minds of librarians in many subject areas.

Librarian positions at some institutions are "on the tenure track." (Note that some institutions put only some librarian positions on the tenure track.) Tenure-track librarians perform research as part of their job, just like other tenure-track faculty members at their institutions. After a period of typically seven years, they are evaluated on their research, their day-to-day work, and their service to the institution and professional organizations. If their performance is deemed to be of high enough quality, they receive tenure: basically a permanent place at the institution in exchange for their skill and hard work. (The American Association of University Professors provides considerably more thorough information on tenure at http://www.aaup.org/issues/tenure.)

In a 2008 study of Association of Research Libraries members (learn more at http://www.arl.org), other land grant institutions, and a handful of other large academic libraries, Mary K. Bolin found that 51.2 percent of the 119 responding libraries offered either tenure tracks with professorial status or tenure tracks with alternative status (Bolin 2008: 418). While these institutions do not represent all categories of academic institution, and while trends regarding tenure change over time, these give an idea of the relative prevalence of tenure.

Working toward (and after) tenure has benefits and challenges. The research takes a lot of work. At many institutions, it represents approximately one-quarter to one-third of an individual's workload. It is typically the largest factor in tenure evaluation. Tenure-track librarians are usually expected to complete part of their research on their own time. However, the prospect of having a permanent job—a lifetime of job stability—appeals to many. For librarians who appreciate and enjoy research, tenure is well worth the work.

Other academic libraries offer alternative research-related arrangements. Some require a smaller amount of research productivity—perhaps 10 percent of a librarian's workload. Some make it possible for individual librarians to negotiate their research loads with a department head year to year. And still others do not require research.

New librarians often feel nervous when they decide whether to apply to tenure-track positions. It's a big choice! Remember that working toward tenure is all about putting forth effort. For those who have an interest in performing research and are prepared to invest time and deep thought, a tenure-track position can be a satisfying fit. Remember that a position doesn't have to mean "forever." Some people try the tenure track and decide that it isn't for them. Others develop an interest in research while they hold non-tenure-track jobs and decide to find a new position that offers the possibility of tenure.

There are time-related limits to this flexibility, however. As a new librarian, it can be tempting to choose to seek a non-tenure-track position and focus on learning the profession. For librarians who hope to move up in academic librarianship throughout their careers, there may come a time when avoiding tenure-track positions may work against that goal. A librarian who has worked for years without proving himself or herself in the scholarly realm may be ineligible for top positions at a library (which are tenured at many libraries). A librarian who has worked in non-tenure-track positions for many years and who has chosen not to publish on his or her own time may have trouble being hired for tenure-track positions. (Search committees hiring for tenure-track or tenured positions look for evidence of scholarship among experienced librarians.) Conversely, experienced librarians who find themselves unhappy in a tenured or tenure-track position sometimes leave for another exciting position, tenured or not, even if it means losing the security of their past tenure. As readers will learn throughout this book, career paths often wind, involving both sacrifices and improvements.

Size of the Library

A number of chapters mention differences in the scope and responsibilities based on the size of a library. The size of a library can mean several different things. Some smaller institutions of higher education have smaller libraries— no surprise. Their small staffs often become close-knit. They develop a certain versatility by handling a wider range of duties per person. Librarians who appreciate the qualities that small colleges offer, such as personal attention and strong relationships, often enjoy working at these libraries.

Many larger institutions have a large central library plus several (or more) small, specialized branch libraries. The branch libraries have some characteristics in common with smaller main libraries. Some librarians find that they appreciate having a separate physical space for their subject area, with resources and expertise all together. These branch libraries often have the freedom to develop an atmosphere that attracts students and faculty in their subject areas. On the other hand, librarians in branch libraries may find themselves fixing the photocopier and placing buckets under leaks themselves because they do not have the staffing that larger libraries do. (Read the Physical Sciences and Art chapters for excellent examples of the pluses and minuses of branch libraries.)

Working in a large main library often brings energy to a job. Students of all levels often come to study and to ask for help on challenges of all sorts. If your position includes staffing a general reference desk or other service point, you never know what you'll be asked next—and plenty of librarians love this variety. Much work in a main library is a team effort. Librarians there have access to a wider range of colleagues' expertise. They may get to specialize more in terms of their own work. The continual buzz and variety are not for everyone, though. Needless to say, all sizes and settings of libraries have pluses and minuses. And no two librarians completely agree on what constitutes a plus or a minus.

Job Responsibilities

Many subject specialist positions cover similar scopes of duties, no matter what their specialty area. For an excellent overview of the responsibilities common to many, see the chapter titled "Changing Fields within Academic and Research Libraries."

One common job responsibility that merits additional discussion here is librarians' roles in the accreditation process. For colleges and universities in the United States, the U.S. Secretary of Education designates organizations that give accreditation. Typically, colleges and universities have accreditation for the institution as a whole, which is assessed by a regional accreditation board. Many individual departments or programs have additional accreditation provided by a discipline-specific agency. The U.S. Department of Education explains the reasons for accreditation as follows: "The U.S. Secretary of Education recognizes those agencies determined to be reliable authorities as to the quality of education or training provided by the institutions of higher education and the higher education programs they accredit. Accreditation of an institution or program by a recognized accrediting agency provides a reasonable assurance of quality and acceptance by employers of diplomas and degrees" ("Accreditation in the United States"). The Middle States Commission on Higher Education, which performs institution-wide accreditation for the U.S. Mid-Atlantic states plus several U.S. territories, explains the interplay between institutional accreditation and accreditations for specialized programs clearly on its FAQ site (see References).

Accreditation reports generally include a substantial report on the materials and services offered by the institution's library. When individual departments seek accreditation, the subject specialist assigned to the relevant area often prepares a report. The time between accreditations for a department or institution varies. Seven years is a common period; however, some accrediting bodies offer longer periods between accreditations if an institution or department scores particularly well on one visit. The Library Accreditation Toolkit offers sample accreditation reports at https://librarytoolkit.wordpress.com/category/sample-accreditation-reports/. Note that the reports cover the entire institution or program, and the library portion will be contained within.

No matter what other duties comprise their jobs, subject liaisons (as well as most of their academic library colleagues) will be asked to assess the success of both their own work and departmental or library-wide projects. Guidance in performing basic assessments is widely available through online courses, conference sessions, and webinars, and in scholarly and professional literature. However, even after a librarian begins to feel comfortable with methods of assessment, the process is still challenging. Librarians know very well that statistics tell a complicated story. In a *Library Journal Academic Newswire* article, business librarian Andy Spackman (2015) suggests that librarians consider using assessment techniques from the business world to help interpret these complicated stories. In an example that will sound familiar to most academic librarians, he mentions the challenge of having to explain that students' need for services at one's library remains high, despite dropping circulation statistics. While academic librarianship as a whole has not yet developed standard practices for performance assessment, this and other creative and practical models continue to develop over time. As assessment becomes a larger and more accepted piece of academic librarianship, best practices will evolve.

Nine-Month versus Twelve-Month Contracts

As you begin to read postings for librarian positions, you will notice that most specify "twelve-month contracts" while a few specify "nine-month contracts." Librarians with twelve-month contracts work year-round. Librarians with nine-month contracts have the summer off, for personal enjoyment and perhaps research. (Nine-month contracts are considerably more common among faculty in other disciplines, who sometimes use the summers to perform research and teach additional courses.) While having the summer off is wonderful in some respects, the shorter contract has significant effects on salary.

ABOUT THE INSTITUTION

Characteristics of the Student Body

Not surprisingly, when they're asked broadly about their institutions, many academic librarians begin their response by discussing the student body. The educational backgrounds that students come with, the majors they tend to choose, and many other factors affect an academic librarian's job in very practical ways. They also create the lively "vibe" on campus that most academic librarians love. While a student body comprised of thousands of students is a complex thing no matter what, below are some of the major factors that affect a librarian's life and work. Most institutions of higher education proudly post these statistics somewhere on their websites. Try Googling the name of the institution plus "Student Body." (See a detailed and spirited example from my undergraduate alma mater, Penn State, at http://www.budget.psu.edu/factbook/ studentdynamic/studenttableofcontents.aspx.) Peterson's, creator of the classic reference guide to undergraduate and graduate institutions, also provides selected, searchable demographic information on U.S. institutions of higher education at http://www.petersons.com.

Undergraduate versus Graduate Students

Undergraduate and graduate students tend to require different services and forms of research support. Undergraduates often receive more group library instruction, while graduates may need more one-on-one appointments and e-mail correspondence regarding their research. Undergraduates often need help with research skills in general, while graduate students have challenges related to in-depth topics, especially in doctoral programs. (They may or may not come with strong research skills.) Subject specialist librarians tend to find that the balance of group versus one-on-one instruction that they are asked to provide relates strongly to the balance of undergraduates versus graduates.

Diversity

Diversity is a factor that attracts many librarians and other faculty members to the institutions they choose. For academic librarians, the pleasure related to diversity often comes from working directly with the students themselves. Students often share their backgrounds, stories, and motivations while working with librarians. I myself worked with a young woman from Saudi Arabia during an instruction session. She shared her dream of eventually training as a surgeon and returning to her country. It's powerful to hear these stories and to become students' allies as they work toward their goals.

Highly diverse campuses often see international students and diverse American students as two (or more!) different groups, primarily because they have different needs. International students may come to campus having had very different experiences with libraries and from academic cultures with different emphases of value put on critical thinking and original research. Librarians help them understand how libraries function in the United States. Even more complicated, librarians often serve an important role in helping international students understand the research process in American higher education.

Many U.S. campuses have special services for first-generation and minority students. Both of these groups may come to the library having less research-related experience than their peers. Unfortunately, in this postrecession era, it's all too common to meet students who come from schools or communities that do not have libraries. Due to socioeconomic patterns in the United States, first-generation and minority students often suffer from library cuts more than their peers. The good news is that academic librarians can make a dramatic difference in these students' academic success. Pickard and Logan's article "The Research Process and the Library: First-Generation College Seniors vs. Freshmen" (2013) outlines development of research skills among first-generation students who receive strong support from their libraries.

Selectivity

The difficulty of gaining admittance to a particular college or university certainly shapes the campus atmosphere. An interesting post from the *New York Times' Economix* blog discusses the practical implications of selectivity at an institution ("What Makes a College Selective—and Why It Matters"). Some of the most notable benefits listed for more selective schools are higher graduation rates and significantly more available resources. Yet many librarians at less-selective schools cite the down-to-earth atmosphere and practical career goals that many students bring with them as reasons for working at their institutions.

Transfer Students

Transfer students are those who begin their degrees elsewhere but complete them at a given institution. Colleges and universities frequently struggle to help students who have transferred from elsewhere fit into their campuses. Campuses often have good mechanisms for teaching freshmen how to find and use services on their campuses, but often lack a similar outreach strategy for those who come in later in their educational careers. Transfer students may also face some challenges related to taking beginning-level courses at one school and then higher-level courses elsewhere; there is often some disjuncture. Transfer students also often express difficulty fitting in on a campus when most of their classmates have already made friends and gotten involved in school activities for a year or two. The news is not all bad for transfer students. Rather, many are achieving a dream despite initial challenges. Librarians and other faculty, however, may need to provide transfer students with additional support to help them fit in and achieve on a new campus. On campuses where most or all students receive library instruction during a freshman composition or first-year seminar course, transfer students may fall through the proverbial cracks and need some additional help.

Commuter versus Residential Campuses

Campuses where most or many undergraduate students live in dormitories have a markedly different atmosphere from those where most or all students commute into campus. This factor is well worth considering when looking through position ads. (Institutions' rates of residential versus commuter students are typically posted on their websites' lists of institutional demographics.) Librarians who choose residential campuses often love the sense of community and fun that comes with having thousands of students around all the time. Those who gravitate toward commuter campuses often enjoy working with nontraditional or mature students.

It's well worth making practical inquiries about work schedules while interviewing for a job. Librarians at both residential and commuter campuses may be expected to work outside the 9-to-5 workday for different reasons. Residential campuses often keep their libraries open early and late (or even 24/7). Subject specialists may be expected to help cover some of the early and late hours. Commuter campuses tend to offer some courses at night and on the weekends, and their libraries tend to support these with instruction sessions and reference services.

RESEARCH ORIENTATION AND DEGREES OFFERED

In 1970, the Carnegie Commission on Higher Education divided most U.S. institutions of higher education into categories that expressed the levels of research conducted. The classifications have been updated a number of times. They now reflect levels of research, degrees offered, public versus private status, and rural versus urban setting. Lists of institutions in each category are available at http://carnegieclassifications.iu.edu/descriptions/basic.php.

Subject specialists at institutions where significant research is conducted often help support the research needs of individual faculty and graduate students, or of laboratories performing research. They may help track down hard-to-find sources from other libraries around the world. They may also need to negotiate funding for expensive resources (such as highly specialized databases) to support special projects on campus. Campuses where research is a major focus often have the funding to consider purchasing these resources, and the time for experts to spend time working with librarians to work out tricky details of searches and obscure materials. Librarians at such institutions may find themselves performing literature reviews as part of other faculty members' research projects. Occasionally, they will serve as coauthors on a research project. Research universities provide exciting homes for librarians who like being at the forefront of innovation in their fields.

ROLE OF TEACHING AT THE INSTITUTION

Some institutions of higher education choose to focus their efforts on high-quality teaching (primarily undergraduates) rather than on research. (Also, plenty of colleges and universities provide both high-quality teaching and research. It's not an "either-or" situation.) There is no equivalent to the Carnegie Classification System to measure the role of teaching at an institution. Rather, colleges and universities that place an emphasis on strong teaching tend to express that preference quite clearly through discussions of teaching on their websites and other materials. Colleges offering a baccalaureate as their highest degree have often chosen to place their emphasis on teaching, too. *U.S. News and World Report* ranks best teaching in undergraduate programs across the United States every year (see "Best Undergraduate Teaching: National Universities"). It provides short, selective lists of schools in several categories.

Librarians who work at institutions with a focus on teaching often find themselves deeply integrated into undergraduate programs. They may serve as embedded librarians, working with a particular class for an entire semester. They may also often find themselves discussing course content and students' research topics with faculty in order to select materials for purchase or subscription. They may develop close working relationships with undergraduates toward the end of their degree programs—or even earlier. These librarians typically value excellent classroom teaching very highly. Many of them exhibit the best qualities of teachers themselves as well.

ONLINE PROGRAMS

Many colleges and universities now offer at least a few degree programs entirely online. For librarians, these degree programs differ from individual online courses in that a student may be located thousands of miles away, and he or she may never once visit campus. (Librarians tend not to make those assumptions about students taking a single online course, although they may be true in some cases.) Most libraries today have significant numbers of online databases, periodicals, and books. However, working with students who are completing an entire degree online requires significantly different efforts than working with students who can visit the library on occasion. Subject specialist librarians who support an online program often create online course guides to help students find online library materials on their own. They may work with an online class's instructor to plan ways to present library instruction online, or to hold virtual office hours for those who would like to consult with a librarian in real time from a distance. They may also collaborate with an instructor so that they can participate with a class through its course site, perhaps writing some of the text for the site or responding to discussion board posts.

Many subject specialist librarians take on some or all of these efforts whether or not they support one or more online degree programs. For librarians who do support an online program, the balance of online versus in-person services can be notably different from those of their colleagues. Besides creating research guides, outreach to these constituents may include participating in online communities, "dropping in to" an online course, and cultivating and managing e-mail and chat reference. They're often involved in selecting and maintaining online services, products, and policies so as to accommodate—rather than hinder—students who live at a distance. In a world where many students are taking opportunities to complete degrees from the schools of their choice no matter where they may be, these librarians make a difference.

Librarians whose work focuses mainly on online students usually develop strong and diverse skills in educational technology. They often enjoy using novel methods for instructing and sharing information with their students. On the downside, they sometimes express the feeling that they lack an emotional connectedness with their students. For some, the fact that they spend less (or no) time working with students face-to-face creates a different overall sense of connection than librarians who see their students in person have. Some librarians, however, find that these positions are a great match for their preferences regarding interaction. Others are able to work from a distance themselves. It's just wise to be aware of this nuance.

FINAL WORDS

All of these factors paint a complicated picture of academic librarianship. Realistically speaking, most of us investigate the opportunities available to us at the time we're searching for a job. We may see 5 or 10 jobs available in our subject specialty—20 or 30 if we're lucky—and consider the factors that matter most to us. We may know that we want to support faculty members who conduct cutting-edge medical research. We may have an emotional attraction to campuses that remind us of our alma mater in terms of size, residential status, and spirit. We use our preferences to select from among opportunities, and then we see what works out. Many academic librarians spend the last decade or more of their careers at an institution that fits their preferences very well. This is a goal for many people—and it can take some trial and error to find a great fit. They learn and experience much along the way. It's a beautiful and worthwhile journey.

The next 14 chapters discuss individual subject specialty areas in academic librarianship, written by experts in those fields. The final 2 chapters discuss moving onward in your career, whether you plan to move straight up the ladder or to experiment with options along the way. Whichever options you choose, all of us wish you an engaging and successful career.

REFERENCES

"Accreditation in the United States." U.S. Department of Education. Accessed August 3, 2015. http://www2.ed.gov/admins/finaid/accred/accreditation _pg4.html.

Association of Research Libraries. Accessed August 3, 2015. http://www.arl.org.

"Best Undergraduate Teaching: National Universities." *U.S. News and World Report.* Accessed August 3, 2015. http://colleges.usnews.rankingsandreviews .com/best-colleges/rankings/national-universities/undergraduate-teaching.

Bolin, Mary K. "Librarian Status at US Research Institutions: Extending the Typology." *Journal of Academic Librarianship* 34, no. 5 (2008): 416–24.

"The Carnegie Classification of Institutions of Higher Education: Classification Description." Indiana University Bloomington Center for Postsecondary Research. Accessed August 3, 2015. http://carnegieclassifications.iu.edu/ descriptions/basic.php.

"Facts about Students." Penn State University Budget Office. Accessed August 3, 2015. http://www.budget.psu.edu/factbook/studentdynamic/studenttable ofcontents.aspx.

"Frequently Asked Questions." Middle States Commission on Higher Education. Accessed August 3, 2015. http://www.msche.org/?Nav1=About&Nav2 =FAQ&Nav3=Question01.

"Issues: Tenure." American Association of University Professors. Accessed July 30, 2015. http://www.aaup.org/issues/tenure.

Peterson's. Accessed August 3, 2015. http://www.petersons.com/.

Pickard, Elizabeth, and Firouzeh Logan. "The Research Process and the Library: First-Generation College Seniors vs. Freshmen." *College & Research Libraries* 74, no. 4 (July 2013): 399–415.

"Sample Accreditation Reports." Library Accreditation Toolkit. Accessed August 3, 2015. https://librarytoolkit.wordpress.com/category/sample-accreditation-reports/.

Spackman, Andy. "Assessing the Ambivalent Librarian: Peer to Peer Review." *Library Journal Academic Newswire.* September 24, 2015. http://lj.library journal.com/2015/09/opinion/peer-to-peer-review/assessing-the-ambivalent -liaison-peer-to-peer-review.

"What Makes a College Selective—and Why It Matters." *New York Times. Economix* (blog). April 4, 2013. Accessed August 3, 2015. http://economix .blogs.nytimes.com/2013/04/04/what-makes-a-college-selective-and-why-it -matters/.

PART I

1 REFERENCE AND INSTRUCTION GENERALISTS

Jason Coleman
Kansas State University

INTRODUCTION

Many large and a few not-so-large libraries employ reference generalists, instruction generalists, or reference/instruction generalists. Typically, these individuals work with a cadre of librarians who specialize in specific subject disciplines (e.g., music, chemistry, psychology) or specific library functions (e.g., copyright consultation, data services, publishing). Specialists are expected to have a deep knowledge of disciplinary information sources and research methods as well as the information needs and searching preferences of students and scholars in those disciplines. Generalists, as the name implies, are expected to have only a general familiarity with the sources and information needs of each discipline. One of their most important roles is to connect patrons to specialists, much as a general practitioner connects patients to medical specialists. Surprisingly and perhaps counterintuitively, a generalist's most important role is as a specialist. The specialty is the information research process. Generalists help students and faculty who identify strongly with a specific discipline to think more broadly about their research question and to incorporate insights from other fields. They also assist novice researchers by intentionally teaching theories and strategies of information research.

To be an expert in teaching the information research process, a generalist must have in-depth knowledge of a vast number of topics including: how to conduct a reference interview, types of information sources, methods for evaluating those sources, processes involved in publishing information in formal as well as informal sources, how to find a subject-specific database appropriate to a search need, how subject-specific databases work, how Google and other search engines work, search syntax, metadata, citation styles, reference management tools, call number systems, subject taxonomies, and local policies and procedures. An experienced generalist working at a reference desk is often able to deftly apply an understanding of core, universal principles so that she or he becomes able to provide substantial assistance to nearly every patron, no matter how esoteric or obscure their need. An experienced generalist teaching in a classroom becomes adept at demystifying the research process and providing students with general knowledge they can apply to nearly any assignment.

Generalists often spend a large portion of each workweek in direct contact with patrons, either at a reference service point or in a classroom. Their reference shifts are typically at general service points where they are likely to encounter a diverse array of questions. The classroom instruction they provide is typically to undergraduates in freshman- or sophomore-level classes who have research assignments that do not require use of complicated subject-specific databases. When they are not staffing a service point or teaching, they tend to be working on creating information resources (e.g., research guides, tutorials, FAQs) for other staff or patrons or working on special projects. Some help supervise student workers or provide training to colleagues. When they are not directly engaged in a project, they are often exploring information resources, reading articles, watching webinars, and asking questions of colleagues. Indeed, the most successful generalists are just as good at learning as they are at teaching.

People who enjoy working as generalists tend to be intellectual dilettantes: they find nearly every topic interesting and enjoy learning new facts and theories. More importantly, they like people and derive great satisfaction from helping them succeed. They tend to be passionate advocates for making the library more patron-centric and solving the intractable problems that persist in defiance to all reason. They also tend to have an unassailable belief in the power of education to enrich lives and enliven minds.

INTERSECTIONS WITH OTHER DISCIPLINES

Some libraries, especially large ones, employ individuals who have a purely generalist role, either in reference, in instruction, or as a combined reference and instruction generalist. It is quite common, however, for generalists to also have one or more specialized responsibilities, some of which are also shared with other library employees. Rare is the generalist who does not wear a panoply of hats of different sizes! Conversely, many individuals who are not formally considered generalists spend a portion of their time serving in that capacity. For example, because of their keen understanding of searching and evaluation strategies, librarians who are heavily involved with instruction initiatives are often required to serve as reference generalists. Occasionally, these various roles are formally reflected in job titles or in position descriptions. More often, though, they live under the wide umbrella of "other duties as assigned."

In large libraries, the roles commonly combined with that of a generalist include student supervisor, learning commons or media center manager, and security specialist. In libraries with combined reference and circulation service points, generalists often function as reserves, circulation, or bill and fines specialists. Even in the largest of libraries, it is not unheard of for generalists to permanently or temporarily serve as subject liaisons, instructional designers, collection developers or curators, assessment specialists, web librarians, social media coordinators, marketing or publicity officers, or outreach librarians. Dual roles with more technical positions are also possible. On the flip side, individuals whose primary appointment is as a subject specialist or as a functional specialist in public services (e.g., copyright expert, data services librarian, scholarly communication librarian) often work a few hours each week at a public services point. During those shifts they are usually expected to function as generalists.

In smaller libraries, roles and duties are even more blended. When there are only a few librarians who provide instruction or reference, necessity dictates that all or most act as generalists in spirit, if not in name. In the smallest libraries, even the director may be a generalist.

On the whole, this degree of overlap is a tremendous boon for generalists and for the organizations employing them. Any confusion or inefficiency that arises when multiple people share similar roles tends to be greatly outweighed by the formal and informal learning that occurs as people with disparate skill sets work together toward common goals. When librarians and administrators with specialized roles occasionally don a generalist hat, they tend to hold those positions and the people who fill them in high regard.

WORKPLACES

Reference generalists, instruction generalists, and generalists who combine both roles work primarily in public and academic libraries. Within public libraries, most reference librarians are generalists as are many of the instructors and trainers. Since small public libraries are unlikely to have positions fully dedicated to reference, to instruction, or to the combination of the two, those libraries are unlikely to employ generalists. Among academic libraries, the larger the patron population and the more diverse that population's information needs, the more likely it is that the library employs generalists.

An argument can be made that specialized libraries (e.g., medical, engineering, government, corporate, archival) also employ generalists. This is true to the extent that any group of specialists is likely to contain some individuals who are very highly specialized in a subset of topics and some individuals who have a wider scope of knowledge and skills that cut across the sum total of the population of topics addressed by the entire group. These individuals may be called generalists by their peers, and their titles may even include the term "generalist." This chapter uses a more objective (less relativistic) definition of generalist that does not include individuals working in specialized libraries.

SPECIAL REQUIREMENTS

Generalist positions are often considered entry-level because they have relatively few special requirements. Most require a master of library science, but some require only a bachelor's degree. Some require experience working in a library, but many list library experience as only a preferred qualification. A few instruction generalist positions require prior teaching or tutoring experience.

In place of specialized education or work experience, generalist positions require skills in customer service, collaboration, and communication. Perhaps even more important than background qualifications, however, are personality traits. The individuals who make hiring decisions for these positions are often looking for people who are outgoing, affable, and engaging. They seek candidates who are patient, who like to help others, and who are not afraid to say to a patron, "I don't know, but let's find out together." They also tend to look for evidence of creativity, broad and well-rounded intelligence, and curiosity. An interest in emerging technologies, a facility with languages, and an uncanny ability to fix recalcitrant printers and other office equipment helps, too!

PREPARATION: RECOMMENDED COURSES

There is a fantastic gulf between what is required for entry into these positions and what is needed to excel in them. While requirements for these positions may seem simple compared to those of subject specialist positions, an excellent generalist brings a wide range of skills to the library. Consequently, the ideal preparation for these positions would entail taking every course offered in a master of library science program, earning a passel of bachelor's degrees, and spending a year or two taking massive online open courses (MOOCs), watching TED Talks, and memorizing an almanac.

For those without infinite time or money, a close proximity to this ideal can be had by taking courses in as many of the following areas as possible during their master of library science program (listed in order of import):

- General reference theory, skills, and resources
- Instruction or teaching theory, skills, and technologies
- Communication theory
- Psychology of learning and information seeking
- Online searching
- Instructional design
- Organization of information (aka cataloging)
- Specialized reference theory, skills, and resources in the following:
  - Government information
  - Business information
  - Health and medical information
  - Legal information
- Information architecture and web design

- User experience design
- Programming languages
- Reader's advisory

In addition to these areas that are often covered in master of library science programs, it is also extremely useful to pursue training in first aid/CPR, conflict management, sign language, basic conversational skills in languages spoken locally, leadership, and supervision.

INTERNSHIPS AND WORK EXPERIENCE

Because generalist positions usually have relatively few special requirements, there are often dozens of applicants for any opening. Candidates can most easily separate themselves from the pack by demonstrating that they have had relevant work experience. The more closely the characteristics of that work experience resemble those of the position, the better. Candidates who have already worked as a reference generalist or instruction generalist will have a distinct advantage over those who have not. However, newly minted librarians certainly stand a chance of getting these positions. Experience teaching, tutoring, or serving as a peer mentor will be compelling to many search committees, especially if that experience is with a population similar to the population to be served by the successful candidate. It is also important to note that customer service experience and any experiences working in a library are also highly valued.

Anyone who aspires to be a generalist would be well served by gaining experience working in a library. If possible, the duties should include reference service and/or teaching. If those opportunities are not available, it is wise to look for any work that involves direct interaction with patrons. This could be a position at a circulation desk, a job helping patrons in a computer lab, work leading tours or assisting a teacher in a classroom, or a role as a phone operator or security guard. If no public services positions are available, it is best to take whatever is, even if it is a role as a volunteer: any library experience is infinitely preferable to none!

Many library schools provide course credit for library internships. Indeed, some require them. Those students fortunate enough to be enrolled in one of these schools should leap at the opportunity to have an internship, even if it is not required and even if it is unpaid. Library schools that provide credit for internships will often help students identify suitable opportunities. Even those that do not may be able to assist with a job search or help find a volunteer position. Fortune favors the bold and the inquisitive: never hesitate to ask for help!

CAREER PATHS

Generalists are often highly visible within their organization. While this is detrimental to the lazy and surly, it is a tremendous boon to those who enthusiastically embrace their work. Such individuals will ineluctably gain a broad and deep understanding of library systems, policies, and procedures. Consequently, generalists who are also proactive, professional, and collegial make excellent candidates for unit- or department-level leadership positions connected to their areas of expertise, e.g., head of reference, instruction team leader, access services coordinator, learning commons manager.

Generalists are not limited to vertical paths: horizontal moves are also quite common. With time, generalists acquire a solid grounding in communication and research skills. Those who augment this core expertise with additional education or with experience on projects and teams become competitive for a variety of specialized positions including those in public services, marketing, outreach, instructional design, and assessment. For example, some generalists complete an additional graduate degree and become a subject specialist for that discipline. Others become heavily involved in assessment teams, dedicate themselves to learning as much as they can about assessment, pursue leadership opportunities on those teams, and then leverage that record of dedication and accomplishment when a specialized assessment position becomes open.

Of course, some generalists find their work so rewarding and stimulating that they choose to remain generalists for the entirety of their career. That too is a completely appropriate path to follow.

PROFESSIONAL ORGANIZATIONS

Anyone who aspires to be, or already is, a reference or instruction generalist should join the American Library Association (ALA) and one of its state or regional chapters.[1] When joining ALA, simultaneously join the Association of College and Research Libraries (ACRL), one of ALA's 11 divisions. Similarly, when joining a state or regional chapter, simultaneously become a member of its ACRL affiliate.[2] While these umbrella organizations do not focus specifically on the interests of reference or instruction generalists, they do provide news and training opportunities that are invaluable to anyone who wishes to remain up-to-date with technology, legislation, resources, and trends that are impacting the entire field of librarianship.

Individuals with an interest in general reference should also join the Reference and User Services Association (RUSA) and one or more of its six sections: Business Reference and Services (BRASS), Collection Development and Evaluation (CODES), Emerging Technologies in Reference (ETS), History (HS), Reference Services (RSS), Sharing and Transforming Access to Resources (STARS). Individuals with an interest in general instruction might also derive benefit from joining RUSA, as several of its sections have committees that address the issue of how to teach, both one-on-one and in classroom settings. For generalists with instruction or teaching responsibilities, ALA's Library Instruction Round Table (LIRT) and ACRL's Instruction Section offer

---

[1]For a list of state and regional chapters of the ALA, see http://www.ala.org/groups/affiliates/chapters/state/stateregional.

[2]For a list of ACRL affiliates, see http://www.ala.org/acrl/aboutacrl/directoryofleadership/chapters/roster.

professional development opportunities and support. The former includes librarians from many types of libraries, whereas the latter focuses specifically on college and university libraries. Many state and regional chapters of ALA also have subunits specifically focused on reference or instruction. Membership in these local, highly focused groups can provide exceptional opportunities to develop leadership skills, form communities of practice, and make substantive changes that help both librarians and patrons succeed.

LIRT, each section of RUSA, and ACRL's Instruction Section are each comprised of several small committees. Members of these groups have the opportunity to subsequently volunteer for membership on one or more committees. Committee members develop programming at conferences, create guidelines, produce publications, conduct studies, and engage in myriad other activities to advance the interests of the section, division, and profession. Committee appointments are highly prized because they provide unparalleled opportunities to benefit the profession, because they facilitate networking with colleagues who are dedicated to the profession, and because they are valued by employers and tenure committees.

PUBLICATIONS TO FOLLOW

It is difficult to think of a group of professionals who encounter as much change as generalists do. Like most educators, they interact with a new cohort of students every semester. Each cohort may differ slightly in experiences, expectations, attitudes, and thinking styles. Each turn of the academic calendar also yields new instructors, new courses, new assignments, and updates to much that was familiar. As reference and instruction librarians, generalists are faced with a never-ending onrush of new databases, discovery tools, library systems, search engines, books, periodicals, and websites. Perhaps even more dizzying are the constant updates to old resources and interfaces. Professional guidelines evolve. New pedagogical theories and tools emerge. In each discipline, the body of knowledge, discoveries, and creative works continues its inexorable growth. There are always new events, memes, trends, controversies, and trends captivating the interests of established and novice scholars. When the world of knowledge is your workplace, there is no status quo.

Fortunately, librarians and educators are legion and verbose and predisposed to sharing hard-won wisdom. They write in nearly every venue and format extant, from tweets to tomes. Although a list of all the sources worthy of attention would exceed the bounds of this book, a select list of sources that are undeniably valuable to a generalist is manageable. Each named source can easily be found via an Internet search. The list includes:

Periodicals

Current news:

- Your college or university newspaper. For insight into the topics students want to talk about, there are few better sources.

- Your local community newspaper. A number of classes require students to research issues of interest to the local community. Staying abreast of disputes, debates, and trends makes a generalist invaluable to students in those classes.
- One or more national newspapers or news magazines. The topics students tend to use for papers and speeches often come straight from the news.

Library trends and news:

- *American Libraries*
- *Computers in Libraries*
- *Library Journal*

Focused on academic librarianship:

- *College & Research Libraries*
- *College & Research Libraries News*
- *College & Undergraduate Libraries*
- *Journal of Academic Librarianship*
- *portal: Libraries and the Academy*

Focused on reference librarianship:

- *Reference & User Services Quarterly*
- *The Reference Librarian*
- *Reference Services Review*

Focused on instruction librarianship:

- *ACRL Instruction Section's Semi-annual Newsletter*
- *ACRL Instruction Section's Tip and Trends*. Each issue discusses how technologies can be applied in library instruction.
- *LIRT News* (newsletter of the Library Instruction Roundtable of ALA)

Focused on higher education:

- *The Chronicle of Higher Education*
- *Educause Review*

Reports

- *The New Media Consortium's Horizon Report—Academic Edition*. Each annual edition identifies technologies that are likely to have an impact on higher education in the next five years.

- *Project Information Literacy.* The reports from this ongoing national study provide tremendously valuable insight into the tools and techniques young adults use for research.
- *The Pew Research Center's reports on Internet, Science, and Technology.* Some reports focus specifically on the public's use of libraries. Others provide insight into how the public uses the Internet.

Listservs

Listservs are subscription-based e-mail discussion groups. There are dozens devoted to librarianship. While some are open only to members of a particular organization, others are unrestricted. These listservs yield provocative discussions and present authentic, often unedited advice. As such they are both entertaining and practical.

- *Collib-l.* The College Libraries listserv includes discussions on a wide range of topics including use of space, reference service, and instruction. The listserv is managed by ACRL's College Libraries Section.
- *ILI-l.* The Information Literacy Instruction listserv abounds with discussions about how to teach particular concepts, how to work with faculty, how to use technology to enhance instruction, and information literacy standards and frameworks. The listserv is managed by ACRL's Instruction Section.
- *Libref-l.* The discussions on this list cover reference sources, tips and techniques for answering reference questions, and technologies for managing reference services.
- *Uls-l.* The University Libraries listserv includes discussions on a range of topics similar to those covered by collib-l. The listserv is managed by ACRL's University Libraries Section.

Social Media

The blogosphere, Twittersphere, Pinterestverse, and myriad other social media realms are well populated with contributions from librarians. A Google search for "librarian Twitter," for example (or librarian plus any other social media platform of interest), will return a cornucopia of results. Since Google's ranking algorithm is heavily influenced by popularity, the list will include some of the most widely read, linked to, or followed librarians. And of course, once a librarian finds a blog or two that resonate with him or her, it is wise to look for a list of blogs written by librarians with similar interests and viewpoints.

FINAL WORDS

Generalists find themselves imploring patrons to ask questions. They shout high and low that there is no such thing as a stupid question. They explain that librarians want to help and that when they are not helping, they have to do much less exciting things. This is because they know that the knowledge they have can make a world of difference to a researcher. It is because they know that patrons can't possibly know the vastness of what they don't know.

Ironically, newly hired generalists resemble patrons. They are hesitant to appear ignorant. They do not want to bother their colleagues who appear to be immersed in vital work. Anyone who becomes a generalist must move past these concerns quickly. Experienced colleagues are a newly hired generalist's greatest resource. A new hire should seek every opportunity to watch experienced colleagues in action and then should ask them why they made the choices they made. The discussions that ensue will almost always be informing and may even be revolutionary to the new and to the experienced librarian.

Even more important than asking questions of colleagues is the practice of asking questions of oneself. Perhaps the best way to become skilled as a generalist is to do one's best to teach a class or answer a reference question, and then after the patron walks away or the class ends, explore what would have happened if another database had been used or a different example had been presented. The lessons learned through these explorations will become the core of tomorrow's practice. When this approach is followed for many tomorrows, the newly hired generalist will become an expert to whom her or his colleagues come with questions.

REFERENCES

American Library Association. "State and Regional Chapters." Last modified June 11, 2015. http://www.ala.org/groups/affiliates/chapters/state/stateregional.
Association of College and Research Libraries. "ACRL Chapters Council Roster." http://www.ala.org/acrl/aboutacrl/directoryofleadership/chapters/roster.

2 PHYSICAL SCIENCES LIBRARIANSHIP

Zahra Behdadfar Kamarei
River Campus Libraries, University of Rochester

INTRODUCTION

This chapter covers the expertise that physical sciences subject specialists possess and need to work in libraries, offering service to populations with physical sciences backgrounds. Physical sciences are subjects such as chemistry, computer science, earth science, mathematics, physics, and astronomy. Library professionals who are pursuing careers as physical sciences subject specialists generally have a background in physical sciences. Subject specialists' work was much more passive in the past than today; in the past, the focus was on collections, with faculty and researchers physically visiting the library to ask questions or obtain materials. Today the focus is on engagement with faculty, students, researchers, the outcomes of their research, and the difference librarians' work makes on the output of their work. Today's subject specialists partner with faculty, students, and researchers. They also embed themselves in the life cycle of research and partner with professors in this endeavor. The author of this chapter will try to capture expectations of today's employers for the physical sciences subject specialists.

Today many subject specialists have multiple subject-area assignments; some have as high as five or more subject assignments. In the best circumstances, one is assigned all physical sciences responsibilities. Physical sciences subject specialists engage with faculty and colleagues by reading e-mails and answering reference questions through e-mails. They receive chat reference questions from faculty, researchers, or students, and they may schedule consultations as follow-up to e-mails and chats. They attend faculty meetings, as well as presenta-tions by researchers. They collaborate with faculty to teach in their classes, and instruct students on the latest techniques of information retrieval. They attend meetings scheduled by their colleagues. They fully engage in strategic planning to shape new service models in their libraries. In addition, subject specialists spend time on developing virtual or print collections and are involved in negotiating with publishers and writing license agreements for subscriptions. They participate in pro-fessional development activities, including national or international meetings to collaborate with colleagues all over the world.

The scientists whom physical sciences librarians serve have their own unique culture within their respective field, almost like a nationality; the subject area becomes their identity and expertise. It is necessary for a librarian to understand the research culture of the field he or she is serving in order to succeed. Therefore the author of this chapter will attempt to briefly describe the different cultures of these subject areas and how these cultures affect the use of library resources.

Chemists tend to rely heavily on the library because chemistry research is expensive and complex. They build on each other's research rather than repeat-ing it. Chemists search databases like SciFinder Scholar and Reaxys. Tradition-ally, chemical databases are searched using words, molecular formulas, and chemical structure. Chemists use the services of chemistry librarians or chemical information specialists to search these databases and to teach search strategies to faculty and students. Chemistry students start learning about the vocabularies and searching these databases from chemistry librarians who teach these skills in their classes. Chemists use the digital and print libraries early in their careers, and tend to involve the librarians in every step of their research due to the fact that searching their resources is time consuming and complicated. Techniques such as formula searching, looking up physical properties, or nuclear magnetic resonance spectroscopy all involve learning and remembering a complicated set of skills. Having a chemical information specialist available makes research easier for them because the specialists have these skills. Chemists collaborate with librarians to build strong libraries and collections, and often invite librari-ans to their classrooms and laboratories to teach the latest techniques of search-ing for chemical information. In fact, chemistry librarians are very much a part of the chemistry departments in academia, and in research and development in the corporate world.

Computer scientists rely heavily on digital collections and are very indepen-dent of librarians in seeking information. They are proactive in promoting open access, and in finding better venues for publishing. They collaborate with librari-ans in purchasing collections, negotiating prices, and recommending resources that would benefit their colleagues. They also frequently work with materials related to the history of science, as well as with older resources for comparison.

Computer scientists care about the latest advancements in computer science and mathematics; they follow these advancements through conference proceed-ings and preprints (articles that have been accepted for publication but that have not come out yet). They often submit articles to peer-reviewed collections of conference proceedings. This process is valuable to computer scientists due to the short turnaround. Papers that are submitted to peer-reviewed journals take a long time for peer review, acceptance, and publication; that is why publishing in conference proceedings is much more appealing in this rapidly changing field.

Computer scientists spend their time in the laboratory, but they also value the library as a place for research and study. They use the librarians' services when they have difficulty finding information. Computer science librarians often make connections with computer scientists by partnering with them and using their software developments and technologies; this is highly beneficial to the library. Information technology is invaluable to computer scientists and librarians; thus the two fields are close in this regard. Showcasing computer scientists' work, development, and the ability to link it to librarianship is a good way of connecting and bringing this group of scientists to the library.

Earth scientists and *environmentalists* tend to spend their time out in the field, relying heavily on their mobile devices to get access to digital resources such as maps. Not only do they use these resources in the laboratories, and out in the field, but they also like to come to the library to utilize geographic information systems (usually referred to as "GIS") and the services of GIS specialists. They are used to managing large and small sets of data, and they also use the services of the data librarian, if one is available. Earth scientists prefer digital resources and still value browsing in the stacks of print collections. They depend on the library for books, journals, technical reports, proceedings, transactions, databases/data sets, maps, aerial photographs, drill cuttings, well logs, rock and mineral specimens, field trip guidebooks, informal field reports, and governmental documents in print and digital format. The challenge for them is finding historical reports, many of which have not been digitized. Librarians can be proactive in showcasing the earth and environmental scientists' work in the library. This not only promotes their work, but also promotes the subject to others who are interested. A library that provides visualization walls for the students to observe large aerial photographs, maps, and environmental videos is considered extremely valuable to researchers and students.

Mathematicians tend to behave like humanists: they value the print collections in the library, and may spend hours in the library looking for classical books in their field. They browse the online collections, but they value what has not been digitized as well, and they like to keep print materials in the library. Mathematicians value the history of math, and are aware of the history of their own field just as much as recent research. Use of preprints and conference proceedings in math is high because rapid access to research is important. There is a math genealogy online (see http://genealogy.math.ndsu.nodak.edu), the purpose of which is to figure out student and professor relationships;. With this information they often can trace the source of a mathematical theory.

The library is the mathematician's laboratory. Librarians can play a crucial role in the life of a mathematician by creating an environment for math discussions and colloquia, showcasing their work in the library, and providing an environment that shows off historical collections.

Physicists and *astronomers* rely heavily on digital collections. The most recent research matters greatly to them. They value access to digital assets, and rely on online resources, particularly conference proceedings and preprints. Conference proceedings publish articles in a timely manner, and they are published quickly after research, so physicists prefer them. They may largely ignore libraries' print offerings.

Physicists and astronomers who are theorists spend their time on scholarly resources, reading, and writing. Those who are experimentalists spend the majority of their time in the laboratory. What they care about is their own creation in the laboratories, and they value online resources. Physicists have been the founders of sharing data and research, often collaborating with each other across the globe. They are the creators of arXiv.org, which is a collection of preprints. Whereas students of physics like to spend time in the library as a place to study and collaborate with their colleagues, astronomers are heavy producers of terabytes of data (such as astronomy images and numerical data); they appreciate help with data management, storing their data, and creating metadata. Librarians can connect with physicists and astronomers by providing what they need digitally and helping in data management, providing storage spaces that can be accessed securely across the globe. Libraries can provide visualization walls, which scientists can use to observe their data, and communication devices that can facilitate collaboration across the globe.

Roles that a physical sciences subject specialist may assume in a library include the following:

- Assessment of resources and services
- Collection development and management
- Data services
- Digital scholarship
- Emerging technologies
- Facilities management
- Instruction and instructional design
- Library space design
- Research support
- Scholarly communication

WORKPLACES

Physical sciences librarians mainly work in academic libraries, in corporate libraries, or as independent research consultants. Publishers often use librarians in their marketing departments for promotion of their products. Indexing and abstracting companies use the services of librarians for assignment of descriptors or metadata or for writing abstracts. Government agencies hire librarians in their research and development for research and information gathering, and for organizing information.

- Academic libraries have been using the services of physical sciences librarians and their respective backgrounds for many years. Universities employ physical sciences librarians where they serve the physical sciences populations.
  - Branch libraries: Some academic libraries may have branch libraries, a chemistry library, a physics library, a math library, a geology library, or a combined physical sciences library. In these situations, you may become a solo librarian. Some larger organizations may have a science and engineering library. In this situation, you may be employed with a number of other science and engineering librarians and work as a team. In these libraries, librarians are typically involved in public service and collection development as well as space planning and optimization of the library.
  - Main libraries' outreach and learning (reference department): In these departments, the focus is on help with research, instruction, and outreach to the university community.
  - Collection development departments within academic libraries: In this case librarians are in touch with the different departments, analyzing their needs, and focus on building collections based on those needs.
- Corporate libraries employ physical sciences librarians to help scientists with their research and development. The corporate libraries are either small and employ a solo librarian who is responsible for all services—collection management, public services, and space management; or they may have more librarians dividing the responsibilities between them based on their expertise.

SPECIAL REQUIREMENTS

Physical sciences librarians can gain experience by practice. Generally, librarians who have a social sciences or humanities background may be able to do the job by taking introductory physical science courses. However, in general, a higher education in physical sciences gives librarians the credibility to collaborate with physical scientists.

Chemistry librarians, however, have more specialized requirements. They need at least an undergraduate chemistry degree and a good command of the field (formulas, structures, and understanding of chemical reactions and chemistry). Indiana University in Bloomington offers a chemical information specialist degree, which involves a bachelor's degree in chemistry and a master's degree in library and information science focused entirely on chemical information and resources. Currently, the university offers a master's and PhD in chemical informatics, since the demand for this field is high all over the world. For this program, a prior master's degree in physical sciences is desirable.

MASTER OF LIBRARY SCIENCE AND OTHER COURSEWORK

A master of library science (MLS) is a requirement for many physical sciences librarian positions. MLS programs offer courses like science librarianship, or science reference, which prepares one for general sciences, but not specifically for physical sciences. A physical sciences background, an MLS degree, along with three years of working experience as a physical sciences librarian will make a librarian eligible for most library positions in the physical sciences. (As in many fields in librarianship, the challenge is finding an opportunity to gain those first three years of professional experience.) As with all specialty fields in librarianship, holding a second graduate degree in that field (such as a master's degree in chemistry) builds credibility. It also strengthens librarians' abilities to work with practicing scientists or science faculty.

The majority of MLS programs offer subjects like collection development, reference, instruction, marketing, and emerging technologies. Today, learning skills like assessment, data management, data archiving, and curation would make a physical sciences librarian much more marketable. Many library schools and schools such as the University of North Carolina at Chapel Hill, the University of Illinois, and Syracuse University offer such courses. Even after graduation, one can always learn additional skills by attending online courses from accredited library and information science schools or through organizations such as the Association of College and Research Libraries.

INTERNSHIPS AND WORK EXPERIENCE

For MLS students on the academic or corporate path, it is always worth asking the career services staff at their library schools for a list of academic and corporate libraries that accept interns. Also, writing to physical sciences librarians directly and asking if they accept interns is worthwhile. A final option is Internships.com. This site provides details on all sorts of internships across the United States, including some at libraries.

CAREER PATHS

In this field, the only formula for moving up is ambition, experience, and education. It is important to get involved in committees and departmental- and institutional-level working groups. Involvement in these working groups will improve negotiation and people skills that one needs (at any level) to advance in the field. Supervising is also a key skill that one needs to gain in this journey.

Academic Librarianship

The next level up for a physical sciences librarian is head of a science and engineering library or coordinator of science and engineering librarians. In the first case, the librarian would be in charge of supervising subject specialists, physical space, and optimization of the libraries. This involves managing service points (such as circulation, and interlibrary loan), managing librarians, and managing the facilities of building(s). Space planning in a library of any size is a great opportunity for growth and serving larger libraries with more employees and clients. There are other paths of employment growth that one could assume after this level. Coordinator or head positions for "reference departments" or "outreach and learning" supervise larger numbers of liaisons or subject specialists who develop collections or instruct, and would assume any of the roles mentioned in the earlier list of "roles that a physical sciences subject specialist may assume in a library." After gaining experience in managing a larger department, one could move up to an assistant or associate university librarian, or assistant/associate dean position in an academic library. The next level up will be a university librarian or a dean position in a library.

Corporate librarians may have two or more levels of growth. The most common path for librarians in corporate libraries is to begin as a subject specialist, and move up to the director of library position, in which one may supervise librarians and library assistants.

PROFESSIONAL ORGANIZATIONS

Professional organizations are great for joining dynamic groups of physical sciences librarians who meet annually. They have programs on collection development, instruction, reference, and public services. Attendees can learn about an assortment of topics and interact with presenters at poster sessions. They can also present papers or posters and be actively involved with other scholars in the field of library and information science for growth and professional development. A benefit that often gets ignored is that publishers are actively involved in the library organizations. Librarians can meet with them one-on-one, learn about what they offer, as well as negotiate with them directly about their products. Librarians also benefit from accepting leadership roles in committees and organizing sessions.

The following are library organizations that are beneficial to physical sciences librarians' careers:

- The Special Libraries Association's Physics Astronomy Math Division, Academic Division, and Chemistry Division
- American Library Association's Science and Technology Section
- American Geological Institute, Geoscience Information Society

Meetings of professional scientific societies will also be useful to attend. In these societies, you learn more about the subjects you serve. Some also have a library division. The organizations are as follows:

- American Chemical Society, Chemical Information Division
- American Institute of Physics

- American Physical Society
- European Physical Society
- Institute of Physics
- International Union of Pure and Applied Physics
- International Association of Mathematical Physics
- International Centre for Theoretical Physics
- American Mathematical Society and their Societies, Associations, and Organizations
- American Statistical Association
- Canadian Mathematical Society
- European Mathematical Information Service and their associate member societies
- European Women in Mathematics
- International Mathematical Union
- London Mathematical Society
- Math Archives: Professional Societies
- Mathematical Association of America
- National Council of Teachers of Mathematics
- National Science Foundation—Division of Mathematical Sciences
- Pi Mu Epsilon
- Society for Industrial and Applied Mathematics

PUBLICATIONS

Publications that focus on physical librarianship are:

- *Science and Technology Libraries* by Taylor and Francis
- *Special Libraries Association's Information Outlook*
- *PAM Bulletin* (PAM stands for "Physics, Astronomy, and Mathematics.")
- *Issues in Science and Technology Librarianship: A Quarterly Publication of the Science and Technology Section*
- *College and Research Libraries*
- *The Journal of Academic Librarianship* by Elsevier
- *Reference & User Services Quarterly*
- *Journal of the Association for Information Science and Technology*

FINAL WORDS

Physical sciences librarianship is an area that is exciting and very much needed in academic and corporate libraries. For librarians with physical sciences and library science backgrounds, this career path is exhilarating whether they choose to remain a subject specialist their entire career or move up the ladder and become a library dean, director, or university librarian. It is necessary to have top-level administrators who are familiar with the treatment of physical sciences collections and services. Lack of knowledge in these areas has resulted in treating physical sciences collections and libraries the same as humanities and social sciences, which has created adversities. Librarians trained in physical sciences moving up the ladder will make better-balanced decisions for these areas of libraries and librarianship.

REFERENCES

"arXiv.org E-Print Archive." Accessed July 5, 2015. http://arXiv.org.
Internships.com. Chegg. Accessed July 5, 2015. http://www.internships.com.

3 BIOLOGICAL SCIENCES LIBRARIANSHIP

Kelli J. Trei
University of Illinois

INTRODUCTION

This chapter will cover the area of librarianship in the biological sciences, also referred to as the "life sciences." These sciences cover all aspects of life on Earth, including animals, microorganisms, and plant life, as well as closely related fields such as bioethics. The areas of research are broad and include fields like entomology, microbiology, zoology, and even bioengineering. Researchers who need resources and librarians for research support vary widely, from those with academic pursuits (including students and faculty), to scientists working in corporate and government facilities, and special libraries such as museums of natural history. Science librarians also serve members of the public, through work in museums, public libraries, governmental agencies, and nongovernmental organizations. This chapter will touch on the library profession as a whole and focus on those skills and resources needed to prepare for a career as a subject specialist in the biological sciences.

INTERSECTIONS WITH OTHER DISCIPLINES

The life sciences are closely related to many fields. Many academic institutions have librarians who are responsible for multiple subject areas, such as environmental science and life science, or health and life science. Some corporate research centers have scientists performing chemical engineering, chemical analysis, genetic engineering, and fermentation science, all in the same building. The exact subject specification in science may vary due to size of an organization, program strengths, and research interests. While many librarians may enter this field with backgrounds in specific sciences, or with none at all, the skill sets described here will be applicable to librarianship in the life sciences and closely related fields.

Some interrelated areas are obvious: biochemistry and bioengineering, for example. Biochemistry is often strongly tied to molecular biology, in scenarios such as genetically modifying a strain of bacteria to more efficiently produce a product. In certain areas of study, however, the scientist studies a biochemical principle with a focus on pure chemistry. The study of agriculture science is closely tied to the life sciences. Large academic institutions almost always employ an agriculture or environmental science librarian in addition to a life sciences librarian. Agriculture librarians deal more with the business of the life sciences as they relate to human enterprise, such as growing crops, animal husbandry, agriculture economics, biofuels, and many other pursuits. Both departments usually have animal science and plant science majors, but they are different disciplines.

The life sciences also cross over into health science fields. Often, a biology librarian will assist researchers studying microbiology, bioengineering, neuroscience, and other related sciences. However, many health science materials are specific to that field, involving clinical trials and evidence-based practice. One field of study that lands between agriculture and life sciences, and health sciences is veterinary medicine. Subject specialists in veterinary medicine will be employed at academic institutions with veterinary programs. Though veterinary students obtain undergraduate degrees in animal biology or animal science, once students begin studying veterinary medicine, there is a strong clinical element to their work, as well as the work of their instructors. This field also produces a great deal of research with animals conducted for the sake of human health sciences.

The relatedness of so many fields is one of the reasons why biological sciences librarianship is a rich field to pursue. There are many opportunities to collaborate with other librarians in areas where the fields connect. Collaboration not only is encouraged but may be necessary in order to avoid overlap in collection development or to aid researchers in an organization spanning many fields. When scientists in different fields work together on large projects in any institution, their librarian is responsible for supporting the intersection of these fields, either alone or with other subject specialists.

WORKPLACES

Life science librarians have many options for employment. An obvious choice is academic libraries. Many academic libraries hire subject specialists in the life sciences, agriculture sciences, and even biomedical sciences. Larger corporations, for example, research facilities, agriculture corporations, chemical companies, and pharmaceutical companies, also hire librarians. Corporations and academic institutions are also hiring research data librarians with greater frequency. These positions may involve analyzing data, storing data, and building systems to ensure security and longevity. Museums often have libraries and researchers on site, and will hire librarians as well. Natural history and science museums, in particular, look for subject specialists with experience in the life sciences. Though less frequent, public libraries are also beginning to incorporate more science, technology, engineering, and mathematics (STEM) programming into their outreach. These larger public library systems hire STEM librarians to serve the community through collection and reference expertise, and tailored scientific programming for different age groups.

SPECIAL REQUIREMENTS FOR THE POSITION

There is some variation between required and preferred degrees and experiences in biological librarianship depending on the employment. Desired candidates often possess different combinations of skills that are valuable in a position. A master's in library science (MLS) is consistently shown to be the highest required degree in job advertisement analysis (Baker et al. 2013). A degree in a scientific field is certainly desired, but not required as often. Therefore do not lose hope, those with no undergraduate science background! Experience working in a STEM library, science-specific tracks in library school, or individual courses taken in the sciences, are just as important. However, a degree in a life science field will be an advantage, especially for competitive permanent positions, bioinformatics positions, and corporate environments. Frequently, these opportunities value a high level of experience working with scientific materials as well as a degree in librarianship.

Corporate employment opportunities may be a great fit for those who have worked in STEM fields and then proceeded to obtain their MLS. In addition to research assistance and collection development, a corporate environment often has the added role of librarian as assistant in intellectual property research. It is not unheard of for a librarian in this environment to assist in patent or prior art (information that may challenge the originality of a patent application) searching. The state of the field is shifting and corporations are advertising positions with different titles, such as "informationist" or "ontologist." Due to the multifaceted role a librarian plays in these companies, some employers look for new ways to describe the position, but at its core, it is librarianship.

Academic library positions also put great weight on experience. A recent study found that the most required skill in academic STEM librarianship was experience in a STEM library (Trei 2015). Continuous-appointment positions, sometimes referred to as "tenure-track" positions, are much more likely to require an educational background in the sciences. In the same study, it was found that 53 percent of continuous-appointment advertisements required a STEM degree. Therefore someone interested in a continuous appointment would gain a definite edge with an additional degree in the sciences.

In public libraries and museums, public services will be paramount. Museums often have archival and rare materials, so familiarity with this aspect of the work in addition to the sciences will be useful. Demonstrated success with programs that serve both scientists and interested novices will be important. Public libraries will require strong skills in collection development, as the collection spans many age groups and reading levels. In all types of libraries, outreach, flexibility, and a passion for the field will attract potential employers.

MASTER OF LIBRARY SCIENCE AND OTHER COURSEWORK

As previously stated, an MLS degree is necessary for almost all science librarian positions, regardless of workplace. It is important to choose a school that has been accredited by the American Library Association and to have passed a review process that confirms that they have met the "Standards for Accreditation of Master's Programs in Library and Information Studies" (American Library Association 2015). Many employment opportunities will stipulate an MLS from a program accredited by the American Library Association. Unless a particular STEM field is expressly stated in the advertisement, a background in any scientific field will be attractive to employers.

Library school offers many opportunities to hone necessary skills to be a biological sciences librarian. Collection development courses will begin to explain the process of carefully selecting items for a specific concentration or user group. Classes about instruction are extremely beneficial, especially for future librarians who do not have an education background. Whether one works in a public or academic library, or a corporate research environment, librarians are consistently called upon to provide instruction, either within the framework of another class or to fill a specific need. For example, this instruction may include performing literature searches, using science-specific databases and software, and understanding copyright. Knowledge of different learning styles will help librarians to best suit the content of a lecture or class to their users.

Many times science librarians in academic environments will be the head of their department, and may ultimately manage staff in a subject-specific library. Even if managing employees comes later during a career trajectory, these classes are useful to learn about oneself as a leader, as well as specific skills such as settling disputes. Additionally, many management classes will briefly cover budgets; a subject-specific librarian in any of the fields mentioned will likely be managing collection monies and this will be of great use. Research methods courses are extremely beneficial. For those interested in academic librarianship, especially with continuous-appointment opportunities, writing scholarly papers will be a job requirement. Even if one does not pursue a career in academia, research methods courses enable librarians to conduct surveys of their user population and to perform other user studies. This expertise is useful in any library environment in order to assess the work that is done, and to demonstrate the value of libraries and the services librarians provide.

Some library programs provide classes specifically for those interested in science librarianship such as courses addressing STEM reference services, scientific resources, informatics, and data curation and management. Less often, library school programs offer concentrations or certificates within the MLS program for science or health science librarianship. These opportunities are especially important for people without a scientific background. Finally, library schools often offer practica (courses that provide work experience for credit) to help those in nonlibrary roles gain experience.

INTERNSHIPS AND WORK EXPERIENCE

The value of experience performing library work, especially in a scientific library, cannot be overstated. Students in a position to accept a graduate assistantship ought to do so. Not only does such a position provide unique insight into the actual workings of a library in the "real world," it also gives students the opportunity to work on individual projects, and hone the skills they are learning in library school. If such an opportunity is not feasible, finding a part-time job in a library or volunteering in a library will enable would-be librarians to perfect their abilities.

Working in a scientific field while participating in a library school program has advantages of its own. This is an opportunity to interact with scientists, think about how they perform their work, and apply one's librarianship to those endeavors. Are there better ways to obtain information for a new experiment? Are there more efficient methods of sharing information and data, either within a laboratory environment or in the outside world? Working with scientists on a day-to-day basis provides experience other candidates and life science librarians may not have, and it gives real insight into the culture and communication styles of these users. In a corporate environment, for example, a library student could assist in instruction of resources and data management tools, or develop guides to clarify concepts of copyright and sharing information.

The important thing to remember is to utilize every opportunity to meld library education with experience. A librarian must adapt daily to new user needs and a shifting landscape of funding availability and priorities. Applying tools learned in library education with real-world experience from either a graduate assistantship, workplace experience, a practicum, or volunteer experience will create a well-rounded candidate with the background and skills to hit the ground running as a subject specialist in the biological sciences.

CAREER PATHS

The career path of a science librarian will vary depending on both the workplace and the individual's goals. In any workplace environment, an MLS combined with a specialization and experience gives one leave to choose a management position in the future. In an academic environment, science librarians are often the head of a library, department, or area of expertise. A subject specialist in the sciences in a public library environment would likely be the only person with that expertise. He or she may wish to remain in that position or eventually move toward a directorship. Science librarians in museums may choose to pursue variants of their training, such as preservation or conservation, or a position in management as well. In a corporate environment, there may be as few as one or two librarians, so opportunities for advancement within a library may be limited.

Research corporations are interested in knowledge management, which includes service to researchers, collection development, and even business and legal assistance. Therefore the positions are in flux; in some corporations, librarians may choose to remain in their position until retirement, but they may also leverage their specific skill set to move into executive and management positions. In all areas of librarianship, science librarians may merge their specific skills and traditional education with newly developing areas to create an individual path.

PROFESSIONAL ORGANIZATIONS

Professional organizations help librarians make connections within their field and interrelated fields. These connections help librarians keep abreast of new accomplishments in the field, encourage collaboration, and provide employment opportunities. There are many professional organizations. Some are general to librarianship; some are broad science divisions; others are specific to scientific fields. It is also useful to consider professional science organizations, as this provides opportunities for librarians to share their input and collaborate with scientists in the field, and many of these organizations encourage librarians to join the conversation with sponsored registrations and discounts.

Professional Library Organizations

American Library Association: http://www.ala.org/
Association of College and Research Libraries: http://www.ala.org/acrl/
Science and Technology Section (STS): http://www.ala.org/acrl/aboutacrl/directoryofleadership/sections/sts/stswebsite
Medical Library Association: https://www.mlanet.org/
Special Library Association Food, Agriculture, & Nutrition Division (FAN): http://fan.sla.org/
Science-Technology Division: http://scitech.sla.org/
United States Agricultural Information Network: http://usain.org/

Other Professional Organizations

American Association for the Advancement of Science: http://www.aaas.org/
American Chemical Society: http://www.acs.org/content/acs/en.html
Patent Information Users Group, Inc.: http://www.piug.org/

Many organizations have local or regional chapters to investigate. Corporate librarians will find it useful to join societies related to the specific field of work their research centers are involved in. It is important for librarians to investigate all opportunities and choose the ones that best suit their area of science librarianship. Most organizations offer reduced membership fees for graduate students, and many provide sliding fees based on salary.

PUBLICATIONS TO FOLLOW

Following major journals in all aspects of librarianship is advantageous as many articles are broadly applicable, and new research ideas in STEM fields may come from those conducted in other subject specialties. Many articles relevant to a life sciences librarian will be found in respected library journals with a broad focus. There are a few journals specifically devoted to science and technology librarianship to be aware of:

- *Issues in Science & Technology Librarianship*
- *Journal of eScience Librarianship*
- *Science & Technology Libraries*
- *Scientometrics*

It is also good practice to follow prominent science journals in one's area of biological librarianship, as well as those journals in which one's users may be publishing.

FINAL WORDS

This chapter has provided information to assist interested parties in seeking out biological science librarian positions as well as the means to be successful in such a position. Necessary expertise and education, as well as relevant publications and organizations have been provided to assist in this endeavor. Still, none of this experience or education will be useful without the ability to be visible to users. Libraries are at an interesting time in history. Less a physical place that stores materials, libraries are more and more becoming arenas for invention and collaboration. The science librarian stands at the center of this innovation, assisting users in successfully locating, ethically using, and properly disseminating science. In order to do this, the librarian must be visible. Outreach is no small part of this profession. It is important to bear in mind that scientists work all hours of the night, and experiments last through weekends; librarians need to be adaptable in order to best serve them, aligning every part of their work and collection with the habits of their users. Librarians assist scientists in their own outreach by providing access to artifacts, books, and resources to the general public.

In addition, librarians are never finished with their educations. In the sciences, this is especially true. Similar to weeding an out-of-date reference book, a librarian must replace stagnant ideas by staying at the forefront of scientific research and library trends. This is one of the reasons science librarianship is so exciting. There are new discoveries made every day and it is a science librarian's job to curate the history of the discoveries as well as to collect new research, to foster the flow of scientific information, to encourage collaboration and the education of the public at large.

REFERENCES

American Library Association. "Standards, Process, Policies, and Procedures (AP3)." Accessed February 14, 2015. http://www.ala.org/accreditedprograms/standards.

Baker, Mary Lou, Mary Frances Lembo, James Manasco, and John Sandy. "Recruiting Entry-Level Sci-Tech Librarians: An Analysis of Job Advertisements and Outcome of Searches." *Sci-Tech News* 56, no. 2 (2013): 12–16.

Trei, Kelli. "Science, Technology, Engineering and Math (STEM) Academic Librarian Positions during 2013: What Carnegie Classifications Reveal about Desired STEM Skills." *Issues in Science & Technology Librarianship* 80 (Spring 2015): n.p.

4 ENGINEERING AND APPLIED SCIENCE LIBRARIANSHIP

Jack M. Maness
University of Colorado Boulder

INTRODUCTION

Engineering and applied sciences seek to leverage existing knowledge to solve problems, often those encountered by human beings. Research in basic or "pure" scientific domains, such as chemistry, physics, or biology, often results in new information that can be further developed toward practical applications, including technological or mechanical inventions or clinical treatments. Physicists and chemists, for example, in developing an understanding of the properties and dynamics of atmospheres, gravity, or orbits, inform how aerospace and aeronautical engineers design aircraft or space exploration systems.

Within the spectrum of these domains, it is also important to note that there a great many related but distinct disciplines. Engineering includes mechanical, chemical, electrical, civil, architectural, environmental, systems, computer, and aerospace engineering—and more. And just as all engineering relies in large measure on basic science, engineering fields rely on one another: computer engineers developing microchips, for example, would rely heavily on the work of electrical engineers, computer scientists, and possibly nanotechnologists to accomplish their work. And some disciplines, such as engineering science and engineering physics, straddle the boundaries of applied and basic sciences. Integrating knowledge from both basic and applied sciences toward a practical outcome is a commonality among these disciplines.

Librarians serving users who work in these subjects, then, must remember that the library users' end goal is often a tangible "thing"—an invention, technology, or clinical application—rather than merely the creation of new ideas or knowledge to be published or presented. Engineers in particular also tend to prefer to seek information themselves; they rely more heavily on personal contacts, conference proceedings, technical specifications and standards, and other gray literatures than other scientists. They are often satisfied with information that is sufficient to solve the problem at hand ("good enough"), rather than seeking all the best information on a topic. These behaviors can be challenging for subject specialists, as their primary role of mediation in information seeking can become less obvious. Tenopir and King (2004) provide the seminal work on understanding how engineers communicate, seek, and utilize information.

At the same time, "the information world of engineering is unique, complex, and increasingly fragmented. . . . The creation of new technical knowledge and the applications of information delivery systems far outpace most people's abilities to stay current" (Lord 2000: 1). Though written at the turn of this millennium, this statement holds true today. Other sciences, such as physics and biotechnology, have more centralized information resources available to researchers (*arXiv* and *PubMED*, respectively). Far from complete, these resources still provide somewhat comprehensive databases that include a variety of relevant formats on current knowledge in these fields. While excellent bibliographic databases exist in the applied sciences, these disciplines' reliance on everything from technical specifications to vendor catalogs to patents means a librarian's assistance in mediating this fractured information world with the researcher's needs is certainly valuable, if not always used or recognized as much as it might be.

Understanding that engineers and applied scientists are among the most direct and pragmatic of disciplinary cultures can aid subject specialists in tailoring library collections and services in many ways. Fosmire and Radcliffe (2013) provide a practical approach to how librarians can integrate their work into the work of engineers, particularly in academia. In addition, assisting researchers in finding known (but difficult-to-obtain) items, educating them in unknown resources, and providing spaces that foster community and information sharing are all ways to add significant value to endeavors in these disciplines.

INTERSECTIONS WITH OTHER DISCIPLINES

As noted, applied sciences have always relied on and at times cross boundaries with basic sciences. Emerging interdisciplinary work of the last couple decades, however, has necessitated new teams that include expertise in many domains, and all these boundaries have become further blurred. Work in biotechnology and alternative energy, for example, necessitates experts in both applied and basic sciences. In fact, many of what the National Academy of Engineering (2008) chose as the "Grand Challenges" for this century are interdisciplinary. "Reverse engineering the brain," for example, involves neuroscience, molecular biology, complex mathematics, bio-visualization, and imaging technology (which in turn involves optics and computer science), among other disciplines.

Work in these Grand Challenges also necessitates the work of social scientists and humanists. "Make solar energy more economical" requires an understanding of economics; "prevent nuclear terror" and "secure cyberspace" will involve public policy, international relations, and security experts; and "provide access to clean water" incorporates some disciplines listed above, but also an appreciation for and understanding of culture and geography. In other words, much of the work of engineers and applied sciences in the coming century will involve solutions that extend beyond mere technological and clinical elements, but incorporate human and natural elements as well.

In many respects, this has always been the case, though it is perhaps becoming more pronounced. Engineers must often manage people and companies, comply with federal and state regulations, and conduct business across political and cultural boundaries. Engineering and applied sciences, because they seek to find solutions to primarily human problems, lie at the crossroads of many disciplines, and their work has been fundamental to the human experience for millennia.

WORKPLACES

Many, if not most, subject specialists in engineering and applied sciences work in academic libraries. But larger (and perhaps wiser) engineering and technology firms also employ librarians, and reference librarians in large public libraries may often need skills in finding technical literature and specifications as well.

Subject specialists in academic settings are often expected to hold duties in traditional areas of collection development, instruction, and reference; and increasingly, in expanded activities that include scholarly communication, data management services, and even instructional and website design. This "subject librarian plus" model arises at the same time that other forces have necessitated the average subject specialist to assume duties in more subjects (Crawford 2012). Some engineering librarians serve entire schools or colleges of engineering that include many departments and subdisciplines. Largely gone are the days when a subject specialist might focus on mechanical engineering because she or he holds a second degree in that field. In today's academic library, that librarian would serve many disciplines and be expected to have a very broad skill set in librarianship.

Librarians working in engineering or other technology firms have also experienced expansion of their duties in recent years. While they may still provide reference, instruction, and collections (which in these environments may be themselves expanded to include product information and specifications, technical standards, policy, and public codes), they are now often also knowledge and records management information professionals. They may run both a physical and virtual library, but also a database and archive of company records.

In both cases, librarians work with engineers and applied science to collect, organize, and utilize information. The work needed to accomplish this goal has simply expanded as the information universe has become more complex and grown exponentially in the last few decades.

SPECIAL REQUIREMENTS FOR THE POSITION

Many positions in both academic and special libraries require undergraduate or graduate degrees in engineering, in addition to library and information science degrees. Degree requirements help prove a candidate's ability to understand his or her users' work and how that work is conducted, and build relationships that are beneficial to the library and the campus or company as a whole. Previous work experience requirements vary more by institution. Larger academic libraries, or those serving institutions with significant reputation and foci in these areas, may require a few years' experience as an academic librarian, even at the entry level. This requirement will sometimes be coupled with the requirement of an engineering degree.

The simple fact that there are fewer candidates with such qualifications than there may be in the humanities, arts, or social sciences, however, leads to many organizations preferring such educational requirement, but not necessarily requiring it. For some libraries, a candidate's ability to understand not the information but the underlying information need, as well as the ability to build trusting relationships, and design, assess, and deliver services, are more important requirements. Often experience working with these disciplines, in libraries or other ventures, can replace educational attainment. A candidate who spent several years as a technical writer for an engineering firm, or as a paraprofessional in a technical library, for example, may qualify in lieu of an educational requirement.

Librarian without formal training in the area they serve can indeed become a master subject specialist. One of the ways in which they may begin down such a path is to receive training on information needs in these disciplines, often through library science curricula.

MASTER OF LIBRARY SCIENCE AND OTHER COURSEWORK

Coursework in instruction and reference services is an important factor in preparing for specialties in engineering and applied science librarianship. Courses on assessment strategies, outreach, and management are also important. Many library and information science programs also offer courses on science and technical information resources as well, which are very useful. In lieu of them, independent studies that enable a student to gain practical experience or study the information-seeking behaviors of engineers and scientists should be sought.

Ultimately, a master of library science program that enabled a student to learn how to diagnose information needs, design services to meet those needs, and assess the efficacy of the latter likely prepared the student for the work of subject specialists in these areas; this knowledge can be augmented by experience.

In addition, the informal learning opportunities that massive online open courses (commonly referred to as "MOOCs") and similar emerging opportunities could become, in the years ahead, ways in which librarians holding a master of library science without engineering degrees can prepare themselves for work in this domain.

INTERNSHIPS AND WORK EXPERIENCE

Internships in academic and special libraries, particularly those that serve engineers or applied scientists, are invaluable experiences. Many employers are looking for candidates with past successes that predict future success, and such internships, practica, or volunteer work is attractive in a candidate who does not have professional full-time experience as an engineering librarian.

Experience outside the library can also be quite valuable. Working in an engineering or technology firm, for example, can give candidates skills in analyzing information needs in these disciplines and in developing relationships with individuals and teams, and cultivate familiarity with the work undertaken by practicing applied scientists. Teaching experience in other classroom or virtual learning settings, or collection development and reference experience in other disciplines are both translatable skills that a librarian can leverage to serve users in these disciplines within the library setting.

CAREER PATHS

Despite a nationwide spate of closures of smaller libraries following the economic downturn of 2001 and Great Recession of 2008, many opportunities to run branch or special librarians remain in these fields. Large academic library systems that closed branch libraries during the last decade often left engineering branches intact, or combined them with other science branch libraries. Engineering firms that closed library and information centers in some cases have reinstated them, or have combined them with other communication entities, such as web design or records management units. In either case, the most common way for a librarian in these fields to advance is to assume supervisory and operational responsibilities for a library-like entity. Managing people, collections, and services is often the next step for entry-level librarians.

Branch manager and similar positions often entail duties that in effect remove the librarian to some extent from direct interaction with users. Depending on the size of the staff, and how duties are organized, a librarian who has assumed these duties will often direct them through and with other employees, both librarians and staff. In this respect, it is important for entry-level librarians to gain experience or obtain professional training in supervisory and managerial arenas. Combined with knowledge of users and their information needs, librarians who manage branches in academic settings or resource centers in private enterprises steer collections and services in ways that align with campus or company strategic directions.

These experiences sometimes then lead, in large academic libraries, to broader administrative roles, often in public services, collection development, or emerging areas of research data management or digital scholarship centers. On smaller campuses that do not provide science or engineering branch libraries, librarians in these fields may often move to this level of administrative responsibility directly, at times by gaining experience supervising small numbers of staff and students, either on specific projects or by the happenstance of organizational structures.

Regardless of the type of library, or size of its umbrella organization, it is important to understand that most promotional opportunities lie in management.

PROFESSIONAL ORGANIZATIONS

There are many organizations that support the development and networking of librarians in engineering and applied science. Academic librarians often join the Association of College and Research Libraries and are active in its Science and Technology Section. Members in this section are often involved in most areas of science and technology librarianship and offer comprehensive networking opportunities. Librarians who focus on instruction often also join the Instruction Section of the Association of College and Research Libraries, in addition to other sections, interest groups, and discussion groups that focus on one traditional or emerging area of work in these disciplines.

The Special Libraries Association is also the professional home to many librarians in both academia and special libraries, and has divisions that are rather more focused. The Engineering Division, for example, includes an Aerospace Section, and the Chemistry Division has a Material Research & Manufacturing Section. There are also broader divisions such as the Academic Division, and a Science-Technology Section that has a focus not unlike its counterpart in Association of College and Research Libraries. These organizations offer a greater mix of academic and special librarians.

Another popular organization is the Engineering Libraries Division within the American Society for Engineering Education. This organization is unique from the other two in that its parent body is not focused on libraries, but on educators of engineers more generally, and despite its name, has a more international composition. The Engineering Libraries Division offers a highly focused membership comprised primarily of academic librarians, but also the opportunity to network and attend presentations from other divisions with the American Society for Engineering Education at annual conferences.

These are the three most popular organizations for practicing librarians in these fields. In some respects, librarians might consider themselves applied information scientists; much as applied scientists leverage scientific knowledge to solve problems, librarians apply information science to address and bridge knowledge gaps in their users and their respective organizations. In this manner, for those interested more in research and theory so they may apply it in their practice, another potential professional membership is the Association for

Information Science and Technology's Scientific and Technical Information Special Interest Group, which is concerned with "the applications of information science to the production, organization, and dissemination of scientific and technical information" (Association for Information Science and Technology 2015). Other special interest groups within the Association for Information Science and Technology can be of interest to librarians in these fields as well.

PUBLICATIONS TO FOLLOW

Librarians in these fields do well to follow not only a combination of peer-reviewed journals and newsletters in science and engineering librarianship, but also publications whose audiences are the users of their library's services.

Issues in Science & Technology Librarianship and *Science & Technology Libraries* are both scholarly journals that also include reviews and editorial pieces. The proceedings of the Engineering Libraries Division of American Society for Engineering Education also include peer-reviewed conference papers, and publications with larger audiences, such as *College & Research Libraries* and *portal: Libraries and the Academy*, are useful for broader context.

Trade publications and newsletters often include more practical advice and current-event articles. Several divisions and sections in the Special Libraries Association produce *SciTech News*, and the Association of College and Research Libraries' *C&RL News* provides related but broader information.

There are many related publications that should also be considered important, depending on the subject specialist's current or intended portfolio. Publications such as *D-Lib*, *Library Leadership & Management*, *Reference & User Services Quarterly*, the *Journal of the American Society for Information Science & Technology*, and other publications in collection development and user services can all inform librarians serving just about any discipline in any context.

Publications intended for audiences in engineering and applied science are also very useful to follow. The American Society of Engineering Education produces several journals and magazines of note, including the *Journal of Engineering Education*. The National Academy of Engineering produces reports on specific topics in engineering, as well as *The Bridge*, which publishes opinion and analysis pieces on engineering education, research, practice, and related public policy matters. This publication is an excellent way to stay abreast of larger-picture issues in applied science.

Finally, librarians serving very focused areas, such as a librarian in a construction and civil engineering firm, or an academic librarian with a more narrow focus, may explore education- or practice-related publications in that particular subdiscipline, which are rather too numerous or narrow to include here.

FINAL WORDS

The greatest aspect of being a subject specialist in engineering or applied science librarianship is the knowledge that your work supports the benefit of humanity and the environment. If one subscribes to the concept of "progress"—that recorded history shows humanity improving in its understand of itself and its world; and further, that this knowledge has benefited the quality of the lives of people over time—then one must recognize that engineers and applied scientists have been fundamental to this progress. They have built our civilizations' infrastructures, the tools we use to make our lives easier, healthier, longer, more rewarding, and more productive. Admittedly, this progress for humanity likely had a negative impact on our planet's other species and our environment over the last several centuries; but it is also likely that in engineering and applied science, we will solve that problem. Alternative energies, natural hazard mitigation, increased food production capacity, and clean water delivery: all these challenges are being aggressively addressed by engineers and applied scientists.

None of this would have been possible without information and access to it. Just as engineers build upon the work of others, both other applied scientists and basic scientists, they could not do so if they did not have information delivery mechanisms—to which libraries have long been, and will always be, fundamental. Progress, then, could not have happened without these subjects. "We," in the sense of humanity, could not have done it without "them" (engineers and applied scientists).

But they could certainly not have done it without us. Librarians.

REFERENCES

Crawford, Alice. *New Directions for Academic Liaison Librarians*. Oxford: Chandos Information Professional Series, 2012.

Fosmire, Michael, and David Radcliffe. *Integrating Information into the Engineering Design Process*. West Lafayette, IN: Purdue University Press e-Books, 2013. http://docs.lib.purdue.edu/purduepress_ebooks/31.

Lord, Charles. *Guide to Information Sources in Engineering*. Reference Sources in Science and Technology Series. Englewood, CO: Libraries Unlimited, 2000.

National Academy of Engineering. *Introduction to the Grand Challenges for Engineering*. 2008. Accessed January 16, 2015. http://www.engineeringchallenges.org/cms/8996/9221.aspx.

"Scientific and Technical Information (STI)." Association for Information Science and Technology. Accessed January 21, 2015. http://www.asis.org/SIG/sti.html.

Tenopir, Carol, and Donald King. *Communication Patterns of Engineers*. Hoboken, NJ: Wiley, 2004.

5 ART LIBRARIANSHIP

Emilee Mathews
University of California, Irvine

INTRODUCTION

Librarians in the arts engage a broad swath of visual, creative, and material endeavors by working closely with creators and scholars. Art librarians primarily find employment in academic institutions (including both colleges and universities that offer arts-related educational degrees among many others, as well as art and design schools, which solely offer arts-related degrees) or in a museum. Please note that, in this chapter, "academic" will be used to denote the first two types of libraries and will call out differentiation when necessary.

In the academic realm, an art librarian usually works with both studio arts programs and art history programs. Studio arts programs will generally offer a variety of media-specific courses and specializations, such as photography, drawing, sculpture, ceramics, painting, digital art, printmaking, and others. Art history programs offer a variety of courses subdivided by time period and/or culture, usually with more coverage of Western art history (Classical; Medieval Western and Eastern Europe; Northern or Italian Renaissance and Baroque; American, Nineteenth Century, Twentieth Century, Contemporary). Non-Western art history may encompass East Asian, South Asian, Islamic, African, Oceanic, Pre-Columbian; additionally, some programs offer courses in non-Eurocentric artistic cultures such as Latin American and African American. In addition to studio art and art history, some institutions encompass or are solely devoted to the related fields of craft, design, architecture, fashion, museum studies, art administration, business of art, art education, or art therapy.

Art librarians in colleges and universities mostly work in public services with collecting and liaising responsibilities. A librarian will work with one or more arts-related departments or schools to develop collections, teach information literacy to support the curriculum, work on specialized reference questions and consult with researchers, and cultivate rapport between the library and the department through collaborative projects, outreach, and attending departmentally sponsored events such as lectures or gallery openings. An art librarian in this context may expect to work with faculty, adjuncts, gallerists, graduate and undergraduate students, visual resources professionals, museum staff (if the academic institution supports an art museum), and other departmental staff.

Within the academic library, an art librarian will collaborate with fellow arts and humanities liaison librarians. One primary annual duty is to identify and justify purchasing big-ticket items, such as full text indexes or databases. If an art or art history faculty's area of crosses over with area or cultural studies, then the art librarian will be expected to work with those liaison librarians as well (for example, a faculty member specializing in African American art will have commonalities in scholarly scope and research tools with faculty in African American studies). The art librarian may work closely with specialized catalogers to describe artists' books and other specialized materials; they may also work closely with staff in special collections, archives, digital libraries, and visual resources. A further goal is to educate other librarians (and other librarians' departments, if needed) on arts and image-related reference and research.

In academic art branch libraries, as well as art and design school libraries, there may be multiple librarian positions within the library; in which case, there will be the opportunity to specialize in a focused set of duties such as access services, collections, reference, instruction, archives, or special collections. For more information, consult the *Handbook of Art and Design Librarianship* as well as other publications listed in the References section at the end of this chapter.

In the museum realm, an art information professional may expect to interface with individuals such as curators, research fellows, education staff, docents, volunteers, and departments like marketing, development, information technology, and of course the public, including visiting scholars, students from K–12 to PhD levels, and community members. Art museum libraries run the gamut in terms of size, scope, and mission. Some art museum librarians must run the library solo, or train and oversee a team of volunteers. Larger art museum libraries (Art Institute of Chicago, Cleveland Museum of Art, Frick Art Reference Library, Getty Research Institute) have multiple librarian positions, many of whom focus on a core set of duties, such as reference and reader services, technical services, or archives and special collections. In extremely large museums (for example, the Metropolitan Museum of Art), there are multiple libraries within the library system, each specializing in a particular culture or time period of art making, and each with their own policies and procedures. Smaller museums may specialize in objects stemming from a particular medium (for example, the Corning Museum of Glass) or cultural milieu (such as the Museum of Latin American Art in Long Beach, California), and their libraries will reflect this focus through supporting collections that directly relate to these specializations. Libraries within art museums can fall under a variety of organizational structures; some are under the curatorial wing, others in education, still others in information technology; each directly affects the library's mission, scope, strategic goals, and support. For more detailed information, read Joan M. Benedetti's *Art Museum Libraries and Librarianship*, as well as other publications detailed in the References section.

Within art librarianship, the three main types of core constituents are artists, art historians, and curators. The artist's main professional goal is the practice of art making. Their use of research materials can vary from the practical (how to make a glaze, how to use a software program) to the inspirational (researching images, historical events, or theoretical stances to inflect their work). While artists need to have a grounding in contemporary art, they have many interests completely outside of the art world—from anthropology to political science, from informatics to cognitive science, from critical theory to religious studies. Artists and architects also are interested in the visual and physical properties of materials, for both inspirational purposes as well as figuring out how to use these materials in their work. Rhode Island School of Design, for example, maintains a materials library for its constituents.

Art historians contextualize and historicize an artist, a medium, a movement, or a museum; they connect works of art through thematic explorations; they use various methodologies as a lens to explicate objects and trajectories in time. Their interests often align with other disciplines such as history, religious studies, gender studies, or American studies. Their primary sources can be images or descriptions of related works, or documents such as diaries, letters, or publications from the time of the art being produced. They will also need to keep up with secondary literature in art history as well as related fields.

Curators share many concerns with art historians, but are primarily involved with art objects within the permanent collection of the museum or being considered for an exhibition. Curators research objects in the collection to appraise (ascertain monetary value for acquisitions as well as for insurance purposes), authenticate that the object is indeed what it is proclaimed to be, and document the object's provenance (where had it been held and by whom, from the time it was created to the time it came to the curator's attention). The issue of provenance is particularly urgent considering the legislation and directives from UNESCO, the American Alliance of Museums, and the International Foundation for Art Research. (For more information, see http://www.ifar.org/provenance.php.) With the objects from a museum's permanent collection, as well as objects borrowed from private collectors or other cultural heritage institutions, curators develop exhibitions to explore themes, bodies of work, and other ideas by choosing objects that make that argument.

All three types of researchers tend to need visually based materials and information about specific art objects. Visual research can be challenging: not all images display exactly what the researcher is looking for; and issues with color truity, size, pixels per inch, and other technical properties can make the image needed hard to find. Online image searching is often frustrating due to lack of metadata (or lack of metadata that reference aspects that are of interest to the searcher). Only a small fraction of the images that could be of interest to an arts researcher are online; and finding images in print sources has its own set of difficulties, including whether or not the image is in black-and-white or color, image size, and layout on the page. Copyright laws regarding artistic images and creative works in general are more complex than they are for text documents, further complicating potential reprint permissions and possible fair use.

Likewise, it can be difficult to track information about a specific work of art, especially if it is lesser known. Two reference tools are particularly useful for these: catalogues raisonnés and auction catalogs. Catalogues raisonnés are a type of publication that compiles all known works by a given artist, sometimes divided by media or period of the artist's work. They tend to be large, expensive, and difficult to replace. The International Foundation for Art Research offers a catalogue raisonné database at https://www.ifar.org/cat_rais.php.

Another tool is the use of auction catalogs, such as Sotheby's or Christie's, which publish pamphlets that describe objects that are for sale. The ProQuest product Scipio indexes major auction house catalogs.

Information that documents exhibitions of artwork is extremely important for all three types of researchers. Artists show their work in exhibitions, which generally are collaboratively realized between the artist and the gallerist or curator. Art historians are eager to track exhibitions that display works that pertain to their interests or explore themes germane to their research practices; curators want to know exhibition histories of works, institutions, and curators for professional growth and for object-based research.

Art research collections are still a mix of print (primarily monographs, exhibition catalogs, and serials) and some core article indexes and digital libraries. Books are heavily illustrated, expensive, and heavy, and tend to go out of print rather quickly, leading to the moniker of "medium rare books" used in the profession. Some institutions have moved or are moving to an e-preferred model of acquisitions; this has ramifications for art collections, which do not yet lend themselves to the e-book model.

Many art libraries and collections have a special collections area to house the more rare, expensive, and fragile works that can characterize art books. Artists' books are a heterogeneous form of artwork, mostly characterized as a book-like form, structure, or idea realized by an artist. (For more detailed information about artists' books, see Johanna Drucker's *The Century of Artists' Books*.) Classes in art, art history, and other disciplines often will schedule a class session devoted to looking at artists' books, an excellent opportunity to get students involved in looking at the collection.

INTERSECTIONS WITH OTHER DISCIPLINES

Some institutions may expect an art librarian to cover not only studio art and art history but also performing arts such as dance, drama, or music, or humanities disciplines such as English, history, film studies, languages and literatures, or area studies. Architecture librarians may work with engineering or urban planning departments. Other intersections are with religion and iconography; with cultural anthropology, folk and material culture studies; and even with psychology (Jungians and other psychoanalysts study images as symbols or archetypes). Libraries may collect art texts relevant to specific historical periods and/or cultural groups to serve academic area studies departments, regional libraries (like the Asian Art Museum in San Francisco), or historic cultural sites.

WORKPLACES

In academic libraries, art librarians work sometimes in the institution's main library (where space and collections shared between many different disciplines) and sometimes in branch libraries. A branch arts library is devoted to resources and services for the arts (including if warranted architecture, design, film, music, and/or performing arts). Branch libraries enjoy a footprint on campus that tends to be much closer to the departments they serve; intellectually, they are branded as a place where arts books are located and where arts specialists are on hand for reference questions. Librarians who work in branch libraries have many more opportunities for liaising, due not least to proximity. Some challenges in working in branch libraries include that they tend to be staffed minimally, meaning that librarians will find themselves checking out books, shelving, renewing books over the phone for patrons, covering student hours if staff is shorthanded, and other headaches involved in running a tight ship. Another challenge is the potential of branch closure: branch libraries can be seen as a drain on resources from the library's main administration; and some departments can see the library's footprint as more desirable as classroom or computer lab space. Articulating value and measuring impact are important tools in maintaining the branch library's position physically among the departments and schools it serves.

Art librarians who work in the main library share space with other collections, promoting interdisciplinary usage, and generally have closer political ties to the library's administration, which lends to increased information about trends, and projects coming down the line. Another advantage is that art librarians there usually don't need to worry about the nitty-gritty details of opening and closing the library, checking out books, and so on. Detriments to working in the main library rather than a branch include the likelihood that the library is that much farther away from the department the art librarian serves and thus that much less on the constituents' paths; users sometimes do not understand where the arts-related collections are among all the other books in the main library; and in general, it is less easy for patrons to use the collections (and can make it more difficult for the librarian to maintain visibility among her or his departments).

Art and design school libraries share commonalities with both branch and main libraries. They house all aspects of public and technical services under one roof; staff whose duties involve reference, instruction, cataloging, and digital initiatives are all together, unlike larger institutions where each job duty may have enough people to warrant its own department. This can lead to increased synergy and a focused mission; however, it also means that art and design school libraries, as smaller institutions with more focused collection scope, have to be more self-sufficient. They will rely on interlibrary loan or other consortial partnerships for materials not locally held (and especially for most non-art-related material). In the institution's organizational structure, they report more directly to nonlibrarians, and thus can run into challenges communicating the work they do and the services they provide to a nonspecialized audience.

Art museum libraries vary from the very small—only one librarian running the whole show—to a variety of part-time, staff, and volunteer positions that keep the library staffed, to multiple librarian positions. Art museum libraries tend to be deeper within the physical footprint of the museum, as their primary use is for museum employees. Their open hours tend to be fewer than those of an academic library.

Somewhat more rarely, art librarians may be employed by art galleries, architectural firms, or individual artists or estates.

SPECIAL REQUIREMENTS FOR THE POSITION

Some ways to develop one's candidacy in an application pool, as well as to enjoy more success once hired, include obtaining a higher degree in a pertinent field, and developing foreign-language skills. An art history master of arts is helpful, but if working with a studio arts program, having coursework in contemporary art history is recommended. A master of fine arts is excellent for working in an art and design school. Furthermore, having reading ability in a second language is helpful, particularly in larger art libraries. Much art historical literature has been written in French, German, and Italian; however, other languages can be helpful if collections or faculty specialization warrant, especially when desiring to work with collections focused on a particular era or geographic region. (For example, the Asian Art Museum of San Francisco collects material in Chinese, Japanese, Korean, Russian, and several South Asian and Southeast Asian languages.)

MASTER OF LIBRARY SCIENCE AND OTHER COURSEWORK

Several master of library science programs offer dual degrees with art history and studio art (including Indiana University–Bloomington, the Pratt Institute, and the University of North Carolina at Chapel Hill). These programs not only offer specialized courses with professionals trained in the field, but require fewer total credits than taking each master's degree separately or sequentially. Barring obtaining a specialized degree, several schools offer art librarianship, visual resources, or image management courses (University of Wisconsin–Madison). The Professional Development committee of ARLIS/NA offers a free e-book detailing master of library science programs that offer arts-related courses and specializations updated in 2015. The current edition of the book is titled *Fine Arts and Visual Resources Librarianship: A Directory of Library Science Programs in North America*. (See the References list for a link and a full citation.) At the time of writing, this author is unaware of any online master of science in information science degrees that specialize in art librarianship.

Some art librarians who have an educational background in museum studies have found it extremely helpful, in not only museum librarianship but also academic librarianship. There are also definitely overlapping interests and expertise between art librarianship and archives (with numerous archives in museums, for example). While the author is not aware of any specialized courses for art archives at present, several schools have programs in libraries, archives, and museums, offering specialized courses and/or a specialized master of arts degree.

If already enrolled or otherwise unable to matriculate at one of the above library schools, other commonly offered courses that will benefit the prospective art librarian include Humanities Information, Digital Libraries, Digital Humanities, Cataloging, Special Collections, Collection Development, and Library Management.

INTERNSHIPS AND WORK EXPERIENCE

Even if not required by the MLS program, an internship or practicum is highly recommended to prepare for the workforce and for the job market. Aspiring public services art librarians will benefit from experience working with patrons in person or virtually, teaching information literacy classes, and gaining hands-on familiarity with collection development processes. For those who aim for technical services employment, creating and enhancing records in the catalog, finding aids, and working with databases will be excellent.

Some libraries have formalized internship programs that have annual or semiannual calls for applicants. Others may be willing to work with interns on an ad hoc basis, or may become willing once a project of mutual benefit is identified. The intern should find several potential libraries and ask for informational interviews with librarians whose job responsibilities are appealing; such conversations can open doors for potential internships. Even if there is no internship opportunity identified through the informational interview, it is still an excellent opportunity to network.

Some libraries offer paid internships, and some offer name recognition; but first and foremost the core takeaways from any successful internship or practicum are to assimilate a holistic sense of the library's operation by rotating through various aspects of operations (checking out books to patrons, spending time with reference, contributing to the library's web presence, and checking in new books); to work on a project that has a deliverable—something mutually agreed upon between intern and supervisor that will contribute to the intern's portfolio; and to engage with the intern supervisor in a way that paves the way for a mentor/mentee relationship, and/or a potential reference once the intern enters the job market.

The internship will be for a set period of time; however, it can lead to volunteer opportunities or a paid hourly position, or the institution may even try to create a longer-term position for the student to continue the work of the internship. All of this behooves a high standard of professionalism from the intern.

CAREER PATHS

Depending on the institution, art librarians have a few different options for advancement. In academic libraries with an arts branch, one can become the director of the branch library. This will involve heightened responsibilities, including:

- Articulating the library's strategic vision, mission, and goals
- Supervising junior librarians, staff, and hourly students
- Ensuring that the operating budget adequately covers hourly staff and other expenditures at a steady pace throughout the year
- Development, fund-raising, and grant writing
- Taking care of the physical footprint of the library, including space planning, collection management, renovations when needed, and security
- Managing digital projects
- Working closely with faculty and administrators
- Advocating for resources
- Supporting his or her library's administration

Another potential path may be to become head of the arts and humanities team. Further, some art librarians become increasingly responsible for collections; this can mean head of collection development, or collection management. This will involve working with multiple people in different disciplines, definitely leading away from core engagement with arts-related information and research.

In museum libraries, one can become the library's director or chief librarian. Like heading the branch art library in academe, this position oversees the entirety of the library's footprint, services, and collections, as well as being the final decision-making force in policy and procedures. This position will often cultivate donor relations and be the emissary to outside constituents, whether interfacing with other departments in the museum, attending public relations events, speaking at conferences, or discussing and justifying expenditures to the museum's directors or trustees. In very large museum libraries (such as the Metropolitan Museum of Art or the Art Institute of Chicago), middle management positions may be obtained such as head of reader services, head of technical services, or chief archivist.

PROFESSIONAL ORGANIZATIONS

It is highly recommended to join—and actively participate in—pertinent professional organizations as a student. National or international organizations have local chapters that host meetings, tours, and other events that enable students to engage with practicing professionals. This can lead to formal or informal mentoring, internship or volunteering leads, and the ability to visit different libraries in the area. These visits and relationships often help students get a sense of how different libraries function, and helps them gain an insider view on challenges that libraries face. Organizations' membership rates and registration rates for students are much cheaper than general membership dues. Many organizations offer awards only for students, including travel awards that help students attend professional conferences.

Art Libraries Society of North America (ARLIS/NA) includes over 2,000 members from the United States, Canada, and Mexico. ARLIS/NA offers educational opportunities throughout the year, and an active listserv. The ARLIS New and Emerging Professionals group (ARLISNAP) is very active throughout the year. Numerous awards especially for students are offered annually. The annual conference offers special get-togethers for first-timers, and there is a New Voices in the Profession panel (those in school or less than five years post–master of library and information science) offered every year.

The Association of College and Research Libraries offers two relevant groups: ACRL-ARTS and the ACRL-IR Image Roundtable.

The Visual Resources Association and the Association of Architecture School Librarians, while smaller than ARLIS/NA, also offer core professional development opportunities, many of them geared toward students.

PUBLICATIONS TO FOLLOW

ARLIS/NA offers several kinds of publications that enhance current and prospective art librarians' understanding of key issues and trends. *Art Documentation* is the biannual peer-reviewed journal published by the University of Chicago and indexed in JSTOR and EBSCO; *ARLIS/NA Reviews* evaluates new books; and *Multimedia & Technology Reviews* covers web, app, and other digitally enhanced tools and publications. The Visual Resources Association publishes the journal *Visual Resources*.

The College Art Association publishes several journals including *Art Bulletin*, *Art Journal*, and *Art in America*. *CAA Reviews* is also a good source of current information. Keeping up with trends in contemporary art is enhanced by reading *Artforum*, *Artnews*, *The Art Newspaper*, *Frieze*, and *Bomb*. Theoretical and conceptual art is detailed in *October* and *Grey Room*. There are numerous peer-reviewed journals and trade publications that focus on particular mediums, such as photography (*Flash*, *Aperture*), painting (*Modern Painters*), architecture (*Domus*, *Journal of the Society of Architectural Historians*), and professional practice (*Art Education* or *Curator*). Keeping up with major and local museum bulletins, as well as exhibitions in the area is also key to professional development and collection development (as well as excellent conversation starters among constituents).

FINAL WORDS

Art librarians work with interesting, creative people who ask for unusual and challenging information and externalize research in fascinating ways. Art books themselves are beautiful, interesting, and often works of art unto themselves. All of this leads to immense job satisfaction among many art librarians.

REFERENCES

Benedetti, Joan M. *Art Museum Libraries and Librarianship*. Lanham, MD: Scarecrow Press, 2007.

"Catalogues Raisonnés" [Database]. International Foundation for Art Research. Accessed February 17, 2015. https://www.ifar.org/cat_rais.php.

Drucker, Johanna. *The Century of Artists' Books*. New York City: Granary Books, 1995.

Fine Arts and Visual Resources Librarianship: A Directory of Library Science Programs in North America. ARLIS/NA. Accessed July 15, 2015. http://arlisna.org/publications/arlis-na-research-reports/145-fine-arts-and-visual-resources-librarianship-a-directory-of-library-science-degree-programs-in-north-america.

Gluibizzi, Amanda and Paul Glassman. *The Handbook of Art and Design Librarianship*. London: Facet, 2010.

"Provenance Guide." International Foundation for Art Research. Accessed February 17, 2015. http://www.ifar.org/provenance.php.

6 MUSIC LIBRARIANSHIP

Stephanie Bonjack
University of Colorado Boulder

INTRODUCTION

Music librarianship is a niche field of librarianship that oversees the services and collections necessary for music performance and research. "Music" is an all-encompassing term. Music librarians can work with everything from classical orchestral music to the pop songs that you hear on the radio. The broad spectrum of music means that a typical music library will include an enormous array of formats and item types. As a rule, music libraries are richer in formats than their other branch counterparts, with the array spread between sound recordings and music scores. Thomas Edison patented the phonograph in 1877 ("The Life of Thomas Alva Edison"), and since then the number of sound formats that were invented, adopted, and ultimately discarded is staggering. Wax cylinders, shellac discs, wire recordings, reel-to-reels, digital audio tapes, LPs, and cassettes are all examples of obsolete (or near-obsolete) recording technologies that can be found in music libraries. This is in addition to the formats in current use, which include compact discs and streaming audio. A major component of a music librarian's job is determining how to preserve and provide access to recordings on legacy formats. Should the music library maintain the equipment needed to play these special formats, even though they may get very little use? Is there another department or vendor better suited to handle requests for content on outdated formats? Every music librarian approaches these decisions differently depending on the collections at hand and the populations they are serving.

One could argue that the most important collection in a music library is its music score collection. A score is the text from which a musician performs.

49

They come in a variety of formats, tailored to use. A miniature score, for example, has print that is too small from which to perform, but is ideal for listening and study. A performance score with parts is better suited for actual playing, with an individual score for each performer and a full score for the conductor. Many musicians like to reference the original manuscript when learning a new piece of music, and facsimile editions—high-resolution photographs of the original score—exist for this purpose. Most music libraries also have an oversize section of the score collection, in which one finds conductor scores and more contemporary pieces. Like the range of music types one will find in an audio collection, a score collection can present an array of notational styles and musical direction. These range from precursors to modern Western music notation to the shape note system used in American hymnody to newly invented systems by modern composers. They also include guitar tablature, jazz charts, and fake books. An understanding of the needs of one's users is critical to understanding what types of music one needs to collect.

Most music librarians have a focus in either public services or technical services. The larger the work environment, the more specialized a music librarian's duties will be. For example, in some large libraries, there are music librarians who solely focus on the original cataloging of music materials. The smaller the environment, the more likely it is that a music librarian will be contributing to the cataloging and processing of music materials as well as working directly with patrons and developing collections and services to meet their needs.

INTERSECTIONS WITH OTHER DISCIPLINES

Music librarianship has never been an isolated field, but music librarians find more integration with other performing arts now than they ever have in the past. Long ago, in the halcyon days of big budgets, an academic library might have had a separate librarian for theater, one for dance, and one or more for music. Now, many workplaces (especially smaller institutions) combine these liaison positions into one librarian position. This is typically called a performing arts librarian, and more and more positions with this title are showing up on job sites. Despite the title, most performing arts librarians have a music background, as the music responsibilities tend to take up the lion's share of the position's workload. Alternatively, in many workplaces, a music librarian's responsibilities will also include theater and dance, even if it is not reflected in the person's title.

The inclusion of theater and dance in a music librarian's responsibilities makes a lot of sense, as these are disciplines that are inextricably linked. Dance classes are typically accompanied by a pianist, as classical music is an integral part of the ballet repertoire. There is a lot of overlap between theater and voice departments on college campuses, especially when it comes to musical theater. Thus one might find a piano major accompanying a ballet class, a voice major taking an acting class, and a theater major performing in a School of Music production of Puccini's *Gianni Schicchi*. All of these students will have performance and research needs that can be served by the music librarian.

WORKPLACES

There is a broad range of workplaces for music librarians, and there may be even more diversity in the future. For the sake of discussion, think of library workplaces as existing in three different categories: academic, public, and special. Academic libraries serve colleges and universities. Some have their own dedicated music libraries—specialized branch libraries located either in the music school or within a larger library on campus. Dedicated music libraries tend to exist as self-contained units, employing librarians, staff, and students. They often have many different formats that they maintain, including music scores, books, and sound recordings. Some music libraries also have their own archives. Music librarians who work in branch libraries, especially small libraries, have a diverse array of tasks for which they're responsible. They often manage students and sometimes full-time staff members. They're responsible for facilities, equipment, and collection maintenance. Music librarians in branch libraries tend to be much more integrated with the daily functions of the library than music librarians who work with a centralized collection. The branch library model is a somewhat typical experience, and many music librarians start their careers by running small, single-librarian operations.

Public libraries serve the communities in which they're located. Some large urban libraries have their own music divisions and employ music librarians to build collections and assist patrons with music research and discovery. Music librarians working in smaller public libraries may have other subject assignments or duties as part of their workloads. They may also be responsible for programming music events for the community—a great job for a music lover!

"Special libraries" is really a catch-all term for libraries that fall outside the public or academic spheres. Each special library tends to be unique and serves a distinct population. In music, special libraries can be anything from a radio library to a highly focused collection like the Grateful Dead Archive to libraries in music conservatories to a performance library serving a major ensemble. The kind of work one does in these libraries varies widely. A librarian working for a corporation may be required to conduct research, generate reports, and do the kind of work one advises others how to do in other settings. Orchestral librarians spend much of their time preparing parts for rehearsal and tracking down elusive scores.

SPECIAL REQUIREMENTS

Music librarians are a highly credentialed lot. A bachelor's degree in music is typically a requirement for music librarian positions. In some cases, substantial coursework in music is sufficient, but the vast majority of applicants come to the market with an undergraduate music degree. Very often, a master's degree in music is listed as a preferred qualification, which is why there are a number of dual-degree programs around the country where students can obtain the master of library science as well as a master of music or master of arts degree. In the past, employers prized a graduate degree in musicology over other concentrations, but a review of recent job posts reveals that the preference has become more generalized. Some music librarians hold a PhD in music (often in musicology), but they represent a small percentage of the profession.

Students who wish to pursue resource description and metadata work will need some language skills. The primary non-English languages of Western classical music scholarship and publishing are German, French, and Italian, and employers are looking for candidates who have a reading knowledge of at least one of these. Catalogers will frequently be working with materials in these languages, so some familiarity with the music terminology in all of them will be necessary.

Most music librarians supervise students from the beginning of their careers, so the ability to give direction to others is essential. While this is a skill that is often developed on the job, one is a more attractive candidate if supervisory experience is already on the résumé. Leadership training can take on a wide variety of forms, from retail management to directing a student ensemble. Think outside the box when adding this skill to your résumé.

MASTER OF LIBRARY SCIENCE AND OTHER COURSEWORK

The majority of music librarian positions are in academic settings, so any coursework on academic librarianship, teaching and instruction, reference or research services, collection building, and cataloging is a must. While there are many librarians who successfully work in public services and have never taken a cataloging course, studying cataloging is still advisable. Locating music materials is challenging because so many of the texts central to our work have the same titles, like *symphony*, *concerto*, and *sonata*, and the same work can be published in several different versions or arrangements. It is incredibly advantageous to understand how catalog records are constructed, specifically the subject headings and uniform titles. That knowledge enables one to better use the catalog and discovery tools to assist patrons.

Coursework in archival management and processing is valuable for individuals interested in music librarianship. Some music libraries maintain their own archives, but this varies from one library to another. Even if archives in music are not housed in the music library, the music librarian is often the de facto expert in the library system on rare music materials. Music librarians are frequently contacted by individuals in the community wanting to donate their "rare" items, so some coursework in rare books and archives will enable one to make an informed decision about accepting or rejecting an offer. It will also help one determine what to do with the items if they are accepted.

Librarians working in small libraries are often required to do some web development. This typically translates into maintaining and revising the library's website, but librarians with a robust skill set may have the opportunity to participate in a wide range of content creation. Courses that specifically target web coding and design will dramatically enhance librarians' skill sets and marketability, regardless of the environment in which they ultimately want to work. An online portfolio showcasing their curriculum vitae, research interests, and social media handles is a great idea, especially once they begin job hunting. Speaking of social media, it is fair to assume that some engagement with social media will be a part of most positions. Many public services librarians maintain social media accounts for their libraries, so a familiarity with the dominant platforms is a must. As a side note: All candidates for professional librarian positions should expect potential employers to "Google" them, so maintaining a reasonably professional persona on social media is wise.

INTERNSHIPS AND WORK EXPERIENCE

Entry-level music librarian positions are not as ubiquitous as one would like, so the key is to log as much library-related experience as possible. Paraprofessional jobs are great for this, especially in public services. While the ideal paraprofessional position is in a music library, any type of staff position offering transferrable skills is a plus. Academic positions that manage students, daily operations, and work flow provide valuable experience. Prospective librarians can also find great paraprofessional positions in public libraries, where they can hone research assistance and customer service skills.

Internships in music libraries tend to be connected with library science programs. The Music Library Association (MLA) maintains the *Directory of Library School Offerings in Music Librarianship* on its website, providing information about internships and practica. If a library school student wants to gain experience at a specific library, it is worth contacting the head of the library directly to ask about work opportunities or other ways in which he or she could contribute to work happening there. Very often, there are outstanding projects in which a librarian could use focused, dedicated assistance to complete.

Within the classical music world, there is the unique phenomenon of the summer music festival. These events typically consist of a summer music camp for children (and sometimes college students) and a resident festival orchestra. There is a prolific performance schedule, and a library team is convened to serve the needs of the ensembles for approximately 10 weeks. These positions usually provide housing and a stipend. Rarely is a graduate degree required, and it's a great way to gain some experience working with music materials.

CAREER PATHS

Career paths for music librarians vary, but a few trajectories are common. Many music librarians get their start in a small departmental library, in which they serve as the sole librarian. These libraries are often housed in schools of music and require the librarian to oversee library operations while also building collections, providing public services, and cataloging materials. That experience is often followed by a desire for something bigger, meaning that the librarian takes on more responsibility within the library system or finds a new, more focused, position at a larger music library. In a similar vein, librarians getting their starts in large systems, like public libraries, may pursue increasingly specialized work, such as serving as an archivist for a jazz music center.

As a group, music librarians seem to possess leadership qualities that make them prime candidates for upward promotion. Subsequently, there are quite a few senior library administrators around the country who are former music librarians. The author attributes this to a musician's abilities to work in groups, stand in front of others, and make one's voice heard. At some point, most music librarians have to decide if they are willing to leave the music environment in order to have an impact on a larger stage. Some choose to remain in music libraries and work toward their dream job, be it the head of an Ivy League music library or an archivist specializing in music manuscripts. Others move up into administration, sometimes overseeing multiple libraries, including music.

PROFESSIONAL ORGANIZATIONS

The MLA is far and away the most important professional organization for aspiring music librarians. According to the mission statement, "the Music Library Association provides a professional forum for librarians, archivists, and others who support and preserve the world's musical heritage." The author cannot overstate the value of belonging to this organization and attending its conferences. There are a range of committees and roundtables that foster discussion and provide opportunities to get involved. Networking is highly encouraged, and there are programs for first-time attendees to make the most of their experience. The association also offers a résumé review service at the annual meetings, which are helpful for students and early-career librarians.

In addition to the national organization, the MLA is comprised of a constellation of independent regional chapters. These organizations provide opportunities for local networking. All of the regional chapters host their own conferences, most of which are held over a long weekend. An MLA chapter meeting is often a student's first foray into the organization.

For those who believe resource description (cataloging) might be in their futures, then a membership in the Music OCLC Users Group is a must. The Music OCLC Users Group is a separate organization from MLA, but their memberships are so entwined that they always meet together. The Music OCLC User Group's conference is scheduled immediately prior to the MLA annual meeting. The Music OCLC Users Group maintains its own e-mail list, which is broadly utilized for cataloging assistance.

The Association of College and Research Libraries has increasingly become an organization of interest to public services librarians in music. The Association of College and Research Libraries' *Framework for Information Literacy for Higher Education* that was released in early 2015 is a timely document that all music librarians who teach library instruction should read. The Association of College and Research Libraries meets every two years, and while it tends to be an expensive conference, the wealth of information and ideas one is able to take back to the workplace following a conference definitely makes it worth it.

PUBLICATIONS TO FOLLOW

There are two peer-reviewed journals in music librarianship: *Notes* and *Music Reference Services Quarterly*. A subscription to *Notes* is included in one's MLA membership. Major issues, collections, services, and initiatives in music librarianship will be documented in these publications, so following at least these two is critical. Membership in the Association of College and Research Libraries provides access to *College & Research Libraries*, the research journal of the association, as well as *College & Research Libraries News*. Both are excellent sources for staying current in the profession. I think it is also important to stay abreast of larger issues in academe, which can be followed in the *Chronicle of Higher Education* and InsideHigherEd.com.

FINAL WORDS

Music librarianship is an interesting field. As the music industry changes and evolves, so do the libraries that support its practitioners and researchers. A music librarian can work with everything from a treatise on the flute to a symphonic score to a recording by Die Antwoord. There is so much diversity in content and format that it's impossible to ever be bored. It is a challenge to enter this field, but for those who feel inspired by working with music materials and teaching others the skills to find and evaluate those materials, then it is worth the effort to pursue it. And there is a network of music librarians to help them do it.

REFERENCES

"Directory of Library School Offerings in Music Librarianship: Introduction." Music Library Association. Accessed June 23, 2015. https://www.music libraryassoc.org/?page=LibSchoolDirectoryI.

"The Life of Thomas Alva Edison." The Library of Congress. Accessed September 8, 2015. http://www.loc.gov/collections/edison-company-motion -pictures-and-sound-recordings/articles-and-essays/biography/life-of-thomas -alva-edison/.

"Mission Statement." Music Library Association. Accessed June 23, 2015. http:// www.musiclibraryassoc.org/?page=MissionStatement

7 LAW LIBRARIANSHIP

Jennifer Allison
Harvard Law School Library

INTRODUCTION

Law librarians are information specialists who serve in places where people require access to legal information. In their daily work, law librarians do the following:

- Review, collect, purchase, catalog, and curate materials for law library collections.
- Disseminate, find, document, and use legal information and materials.
- Teach people how to conduct legal research.

Although law librarianship in the United States has evolved over the last 100-plus years, certain core responsibilities, performed in a particular order, have always been at the heart of the profession. Robert C. Berring, who served as the director of the University of California–Berkeley Law Library, described it this way: "First, they gathered materials. Second, they created records of the materials that were so gathered. As a part of this process they developed schemes for organizing information so that it could be retrieved. Third, they physically arranged and preserved the materials. Fourth, they distributed the materials to those who needed them" (Berring 2012: 71).

The Roles and Responsibilities of Law Librarians

Reference, research, and public services law librarians work directly with library users. They answer reference questions in person at the reference desk, as well as by phone, e-mail, and online chat. They also provide research assistance by creating research guides and bibliographies, and by offering research consultation meetings and training classes.

Some research librarians are subject specialists. Many law libraries, for example, have one or more librarians who specialize in foreign, comparative, and international law. Foreign, comparative, and international law focuses on the laws of other countries (non-U.S. law for American law librarians), and international law (laws and legal principles that govern relationships between nations) (Rumsey 2006).

Other public-facing roles for law librarians focus on targeted interactions with library users. A student services librarian in an academic law library, for example, may organize legal research workshops for law students researching seminar paper topics, editing law journals, or preparing to work as summer interns. Similarly, faculty services librarians at law school libraries provide support for law professors, including creating training programs for faculty research assistants and managing Internet portals for faculty scholarship (Jayasuriya and Brillantine 2007; Schlit 2007).

Behind the scenes, acquisitions and collection development librarians focus on building and maintaining the library's collection (Lenz and Wohl 2008). In technical services, professional librarians work as catalogers and bibliographers (see issues of *Technical Services Law Librarian* for more information). In addition, some law libraries have archivists and other professional librarians who manage special and rare collections (see issues of "LH & RB Newsletter" for more information).

Law Librarianship, Legal Materials, and Legal Research Skills

Legal information is not only voluminous, but it is also organized in a unique way. This can overwhelm the most seasoned researcher, let alone a first-year law student. Therefore the work of law librarians as legal research facilitators and teachers is very important.

Organizationally, legal materials fall under one of two classifications. Primary materials are "the law" issued by government entities, including legislation, regulations, and judicial opinions. There is also an enormous body of secondary materials, including treatises, legal periodicals, and legal reference works (including dictionaries and encyclopedias), which help researchers find and analyze primary law.

Legal materials are available both in print and electronically, both for free online and through subscription databases like WestlawNext, Lexis Advance, and HeinOnline. In recent years, more and more legal materials have been made available through various digital formats. In 2010, John Palfrey, at the time the vice dean of information resources at Harvard Law School, described the world of legal information as "digital-plus" (Palfrey 2010: 172). New legal resources may primarily be published in digital format; however, because legal research is still done in books as well as online, "print and other analog formats will not disappear" (Palfrey 2010: 175). A major challenge of law librarianship is to know and understand this changing landscape sufficiently well to guide information seekers of all backgrounds and research abilities.

Palfrey also cites digital nativism as a unique challenge to modern law librarianship. Although young people "feel very comfortable in digital information environments" (176), they also have digital research habits that are less effective for legal research, such as "simple keyword searches learned through Google searching" (177). Accordingly, law librarians must "figure out which information-seeking practices to reinforce and which to correct during a period of rapid change in user behavior" (177). Palfrey is clear: "Never before have law librarians been more necessary than during this period of transition" (177).

The American Association of Law Libraries (AALL) is the major professional organization for law librarians in the United States. It takes seriously the challenges described by Palfrey, as well as criticism of the legal research skills of law students and young attorneys in the scholarly literature on legal research. In 2013, the AALL executive board approved a framework for legal research competency that defines the values that are critical to conducting skilled legal research (see "Principles and Standards for Legal Research Competency" at http://www.aallnet.org/mm/Advocacy/recommendedguidelines/policy-legal rescompetency.html). These values are reflected in the five principles for legal research competency, as defined in the framework.

The framework also outlines the specific skills that are necessary to demonstrate legal research competency, and provides a way to measure mastery of those skills. It serves as an important guideline to law librarians as they define and deliver library services.

The Unauthorized Practice of Law

The unauthorized practice of law is a specific concern in law librarianship, especially when it comes to assisting nonlawyers representing themselves in a legal dispute (these people are often referred to as "pro se patrons") (Hale-Janeke and Blackburn 2008). While some law librarians have law degrees and are licensed to practice law, law librarians are not permitted to offer legal advice when providing research assistance in a library setting.

Many law librarians struggle with this, as there is not a universally accepted definition of what "legal advice" is. AALL does provide some guidance on dealing with this issue (see "Unauthorized Practice of Law Toolkit"). However, the general rule that law librarians follow is to err on the side of caution, which becomes easier with more experience handling reference inquires. In the end, law librarians provide tools and guidance for people looking for legal information, but are not allowed to help patrons interpret legal materials.

INTERSECTIONS WITH OTHER DISCIPLINES

Although American law librarians have their own professional organization, and are generally not as involved with the American Library Association as librarians in other disciplines, still law librarians value the same things as other librarians. A good illustration of these shared values are the "Key Action Areas" defined by the American Library Association found online at http://www.ala.org/aboutala/missionpriorities/keyactionareas.

Law librarianship literature directly addresses these themes. Of particular interest is how legal issues impact information access in law libraries. Academic law library director D. R. Jones wrote in 2013 of how digital expansion has changed how copyright holders allow libraries to purchase and provide access to electronic materials, primarily in terms of significant pricing increases and restrictions on lending and borrowing (Jones 2013). Similarly, collection development and information access can also be impacted by First Amendment law. Anne Klinefelter, another academic law library director, published an analytical survey of First Amendment case law in 2010. The purpose of this survey was to educate publicly funded law libraries on potential limits to their discretion in determining which materials to purchase and how to provide access to the Internet (Klinefelter 2010). Both of these issues raise serious concerns for law libraries and the researchers who depend on them for complete, current collections of relevant legal materials.

Other American Library Association Key Action Areas are also discussed in the law librarianship literature. For example, the AALL's *Law Library Journal* features a regular column on diversity, *Diversity Dialogues* . . . . In the Summer 2014 issue, columnist Ronald Wheeler proposed expanding the definition of diversity beyond considerations of race, ethnicity, gender and gender identity, and sexual orientation, and discussed how diverse professional interests and aptitudes (such as writing and technology), as well as life and cultural experiences, have enriched and strengthened law librarianship as a profession (Wheeler 2014).

WORKPLACES

Law librarians work in law libraries, law firms, courts, public libraries—anyplace where information professionals are needed to help collect and disseminate information about the law to people who require it. Some law librarians do not work in law libraries at all, as their skills are useful for positions in academic administration, legal publishing, and legal information product development (Wheeler 2014: 137).

Academic Law Libraries

Academic law libraries are affiliated with law schools. They maintain a physical and/or virtual location for law school affiliates (and, in some cases, university affiliates and the general public) that is suitable and has sufficient materials for legal study and research. In addition, an academic law library provides various forms of services and support, including research assistance and instruction, for the law school's legal scholarship and academic programs.

While a student at the University of Buffalo, Theodora Belniak wrote a fascinating (and award-winning) 2009 article about the historical development of law librarianship. She characterized the academic law librarian of the early 1900s, based on the literary evidence from the period, as "the superman of the law school library" (Belniak 2009: 433), who combined extensive knowledge of the library's unique collection, a deep understanding of legal science, and finely honed teaching skills to serve not only law school affiliates but also the public at large.

During the latter half of the twentieth century, the nature of academic law librarianship changed. Belniak attributed these changes to new developments in legal publishing, legal information delivery, the typical law school curriculum, and professional qualification standards. These factors influence academic law librarianship to this day, as law school librarians are expected to be extensively educated, knowledgeable of legal bibliography (the methods and practice by which legal research materials are selected, cataloged, curated, described, and searched for), and technically savvy. They are also expected to keep abreast of developments in the field through professional reading and by participating in organizations like AALL.

Government Law Libraries

This category includes libraries maintained by federal, state, and local governments that serve the legal research needs of government employees (judges and government attorneys) and, in some cases, practicing attorneys and the general public. Government law libraries serve many types of organizations, including courts, legislatures, administrative agencies, and correctional facilities.

The AALL State, Court & County Law Libraries Special Interest Section) has established standards for county public law libraries. According to these standards, these libraries are created and governed by statutory mandates, and their goals and missions are to reflect these mandates. They are to be staffed by "professional personnel," and they must be "conveniently located" to ensure access by legal researcher. These libraries also must provide sufficient "information services" (including Internet access) and a complete, up-to-date collection of the jurisdiction's primary legal materials ("State, Court & County Law Libraries Special Interest Section, County Public Law Library Standards: April, 2009").

Private Law Libraries

Some law firms have libraries that are staffed by professional librarians. A law firm librarian provides many of the same services as academic and government librarians, including research assistance and instruction and collection development and maintenance. However, the value of a law firm librarian is, in some ways, measured differently than in academic or government law libraries.

Whereas law schools generally have unlimited access to legal subscription databases like WestlawNext, that would be cost prohibitive for a law firm. Although law firms do subscribe to these databases, they generally have an arrangement in which they pay a fee for each document viewed. A common horror story that legal research professors tell law students is of a luckless first-year associate, fresh out of law school, racking up thousands of dollars in Westlaw charges during his early days at the firm.

Law firm librarians can help and teach the firm's attorneys the most cost-effective and efficient ways to conduct legal research, and can tailor this instruction and assistance specifically to the firm's resources and the type of work the firm does for clients. Any cost savings realized by this service can be passed directly on to the firm's clients, thereby helping to ensure client retention.

In the end, law firm librarians are a great resource for young associates. Jenny Selby, who went on to work as a reference librarian at the University of Michigan Law School, recalled how grateful she was for the librarian's help when she was a young lawyer at a midsize firm early in her career: "Many times, she helped me craft effective searches for expensive online databases ... saving me from looking bad by racking up too much in online searching costs" (University of Michigan Law School 2011).

For more information about private law libraries, see the website of the AALL Private Law Libraries Special Interest Section at http://www.aallnet.org/sections/pll.

MASTER OF LIBRARY SCIENCE AND OTHER COURSEWORK

In general, professional law librarians have completed, or are in the process of completing, a master of library science degree. According to AALL, "the overwhelming majority of those working as law librarians" have a master of library science ("Education Requirements"). While some library schools offer dedicated law librarianship programs, all master of library science programs provide compulsory instruction on the skills that law librarians need, such as information classification, reference, and library management. Elective courses, especially those in which students practice working with legal materials (such as government documents), can also provide valuable training and knowledge for future law librarians.

A long-standing debate among American law librarians is the value of having studied law and earned a juris doctor (JD) degree (Bonney 1991; Whisner 2008). According to the AALL's Education Requirements, "about one-third of all law librarians also have law degrees, ... but fewer than 20% of law librarian positions being filled require both degrees" ("Education Requirements"). The librarian's role and the type of law library can greatly influence any formal or informal requirement for both degrees. In 2014, librarian James M. Donovan published a survey of 2010–11 AALL membership demographic data concerning the educational qualifications of law librarians. Based on his analysis of the survey results, in which he found that 57.8 percent of academic law librarians hold both degrees (although this number is significantly lower for nonacademic law librarians, at only 18.6 percent) (Donovan 2014: 30), he concluded that "anyone who aspires to become a law librarian will have a major hurdle to overcome without a JD [juris doctor], especially if aiming for a public services position within an academic setting" (Donovan 2014: 2).

For law librarians with particular subspecialties, additional educational credentials may also be recommended, if not required. For example, foreign, comparative, and international law librarians may have specialized knowledge of foreign legal systems and languages (Rumsey 2006).

A law librarian with an active state bar admission may have to fulfill continuing legal education requirements. Continuing legal education requirements vary by state. For example, the State Bar of California requires attorneys with active memberships to complete 25 hours of continuing legal education every three years ("MCLE Requirements"). While there are no formal continuing legal education requirements for law librarians, opportunities for continuing education are numerous, from print and electronic publications to conferences, workshops, and training classes. Topics of interest include new developments in legal bibliography and law-related advancements in technology, especially those concerning heavily used electronic resources like WestlawNext (Balleste 2007; Wheeler 2011).

Many law librarians also contribute to the scholarly literature of librarianship and law, and present at professional conferences. This aids in the development of their research, writing, public speaking, and collaboration skills. It also allows them to contribute to a body of knowledge that those who follow them can draw on to assess where the profession has been, and how it should evolve.

INTERNSHIPS AND WORK EXPERIENCE

As in other areas of librarianship, those who aspire to be law librarians must study, work, and prepare strategically in order to land that first professional job. Internships, undertaken during law school, library school, or both, can be an important aspect of this strategic preparation.

An intern may shadow a reference librarian on the reference desk, write a research guide or bibliography on a topic that library users frequently ask about, or process and catalog legal materials in technical services. By performing these tasks, an intern can gain real-world knowledge about law libraries, as well as practical skills that make him or her much more employable after graduation, whether or not the internship leads directly to a full-time job. This knowledge and experience, communicated through one's résumé, cover letter, and interview, can give a job seeker an important edge: it instills confidence in the hiring manager that the person is ready to hit the ground running and immediately contribute in a meaningful way.

CAREER PATHS

Some law librarians enjoy their work so much that they choose to remain reference librarians or catalogers their entire career. However, as with any other profession, professional advancement is also possible.

At the head of the law library is the law library director, who has two major responsibilities: (1) overseeing the administration of the law library, and (2) managing the law library's relationship with the law school and university communities. Many law library directors have several years of experience as law librarians. Lynne Maxwell, the newly appointed director of the law library at the West Virginia University College of Law, described how this experience helped her establish the four "resolutions" she would follow as a library director: (1) listening to library employees, (2) communicating with library employees, (3) protecting library employees from "potential abuse" by the rest of the law school community, and (4) respecting the "world" of library employees. These resolutions provide a succinct outline of her responsibilities as head of the library, and how to best carry them out (Maxwell 2013).

Law libraries can also have intermediate management positions heading various departments, such as head of reference, head of technical services (this department generally includes cataloging and acquisitions), and head of public services. Department-level managers manage their direct reports, establish policies and procedures, and represent their departments in library-wide management and planning activities.

In addition to employment experience, important qualifications for professional advancement include attending and presenting at professional conferences, involvement with professional organizations such as AALL, participating in library committees, and scholarly research and publication.

PROFESSIONAL ORGANIZATIONS

In the United States, the major professional organization for law librarians is AALL. AALL holds a national meeting once a year, during which law librarians come together for networking and educational events. Within AALL are special interest sections and regional chapters. A directory of AALL's special interest section websites is available at http://www.aallnet.org/mm/Member-Communities/sis/sis-websites. A list of AALL's 31 regional chapters is available at http://www.aallnet.org/mm/Member-Communities/chapters. Many U.S. law librarians who specialize in foreign and international law are also members of the International Association of Law Libraries.

Some law librarians are also involved in library organizations that do not focus exclusively on law librarians, including the American Library Association, the Association of College and Research Libraries, and the Special Libraries Association.

PUBLICATIONS TO FOLLOW

Primary among the periodicals devoted exclusively to American law librarianship are the AALL publications: *Law Library Journal*, which features scholarly articles, and *AALL Spectrum*, which publishes feature-length works. AALL Special Interest Sections and regional chapters also publish newsletters.

There are also journals that focus primarily on topics within law librarianship. *Legal Reference Services Quarterly* publishes articles of particular interest to law librarians who work in research and reference services. Another example of this type of publication is Hein's *Trends in Law Library Management and Technology*.

The *International Journal of Legal Information*, published by the International Association of Law Libraries, presents information about law librarianship from around the world, including the United States. Scholarly publications of some non-U.S. law librarianship organizations may also be of interest to American law librarians. Examples of journals from foreign law library associations that may publish articles of interest to American law librarians include the British and Irish Association of Law Librarians' *Legal Information Management*, and the Canadian Association of Law Libraries' *Canadian Law Library Review*. Non-English-language law librarianship journals also feature interesting and informative content. For example, Germany's professional organization for law librarians, the Arbeitsgemeinschaft für juristisches Bibliotheks- und Dokumentationswesen, publishes a German-language journal, *Recht, Bibliothek, Dokumentation—RBD*, three times per year.

General and subject-specific law reviews also publish content relevant to the work of law librarians, especially those that discuss teaching legal research, legal research methodology, and legal practice. (Examples of recent law review articles that may be of particular interest to law librarians, covering such topics as legal pedagogy, legal research, and professional responsibility, include Peoples 2013; Feliu and Frazer 2012; Dow 2011; Bekhruz 2010; Buckingham 2009; and Otey 2013.)

In addition, state bar journals also often include articles about legal research that law librarians may find to be informative. An example of a recent bar journal articles that may be of interest to law librarians include Ruth S. Stevens's "Legal Research: Is There an App for That?" (2012).

FINAL WORDS

Law librarianship can be a very rewarding career choice. Navigating the legal system is complicated for anyone who does not have experience doing so, and yet access to legal information is a critical component of the justice system. Because of the work they do, law librarians provide a unique and valuable service to a wide variety of people. The educational path toward a career in law librarianship can be long, especially if it includes three years of law school. Furthermore, law librarians' salaries are not as high as those of many practicing attorneys. However, the hours are good, the work is interesting and varied, and there is a real sense of purpose and service in law librarianship, which definitely has its own rewards.

REFERENCES

"About ALA: Key Action Areas." American Library Association. Accessed April 19, 2015. http://www.ala.org/aboutala/.

Balleste, Roy. "Technology Trends in Law Libraries." In *Law Librarianship for the Twenty-First Century*, ed. Roy Balleste, Sonia Luna-Lamas, and Lisa Smith-Butler. Lanham, MD: Scarecrow Press, 2007.

Bekhruz, K. N. "Comparative Legal Research in an Era of Globalization." *Journal of Comparative Law* 5, no. 1 (2010): 94–107.

Belniak, Theodora. "The Law Librarian of the Twentieth and Twenty-First Centuries: A Figure in Flux." *Law Library Journal* 101, no. 4 (2009): 427–49.

Berring, Robert C. "The End of Scholarly Bibliography: Reconceptualizing Law Librarianship." *Law Library Journal* 104, no. 1 (2012): 69–82.

Bonney, Barbara B. "The Controversy over Dual Degrees for Law Librarians." *Legal Reference Services Quarterly* 11, no. 1 (1991): 127–33.

Buckingham, Richard. "Thinking Like a Librarian: Tips for Better Legal Research." *Thomas M. Cooley Journal of Practical and Clinical Law* 12, no. 1 (2009): 1–24.

"Chapters." *American Association of Law Libraries*. Accessed July 7, 2015. http://www.aallnet.org/mm/Member-Communities/chapters.

Donovan, James M. "Order Matters: Typology of Dual-Degreed Law Librarians." *Legal Reference Services Quarterly* 33, no. 1 (2014): 1–37.

Dow, Steven B. "Rethinking Legal Research: Preparing Law Students for Using Empirical Data." *Michigan State Law Review* , no. 3 (2011): 523–72.

"Education Requirements." *American Association of Law Libraries*. Accessed April 19, 2015. http://www.aallnet.org/mm/Careers/lawlibrarycareers/Education-Requirements.

Feliu, Vincenc, and Helen Frazer. "Embedded Librarians: Teaching Legal Research as a Lawyering Skill." *Journal of Legal Education* 61, no. 4 (2012): 540–59.

Hale-Janeke, Amy, and Sharon Blackburn. "Law Librarians and the Self-Represented Litigant." *Legal Reference Services Quarterly* 27, no. 1 (2008): 65–88.

Jayasuriya, H. Kumar Percy, and Frances M. Brillantine. "Student Services in the 21st Century: Evolution and Innovation in Discovering Student Needs, Teaching Information Literacy, and Designing Library, 2.0-Based Student Services." *Legal Reference Services Quarterly* 26, nos. 1–2 (2007): 135–70.

Jones, D. R. "Locked Collections: Copyright and the Future of Research Support." *Law Library Journal* 105, no. 4 (2013): 425–60.

Klinefelter, Anne. "First Amendment Limits on Library Collection Management." *Law Library Journal* 102, no. 3 (2010): 343–74.

Lenz, Connie, and Helen Wohl. "Does Form Follow Function? Academic Law Libraries' Organizational Structures for Collection Development." *Law Library Journal* 100, no. 1 (2008): 59–116.

Maxwell, Lynne F. "Coming into the Country: Resolutions of a New Law Library Director." *Law Library Journal* 105, no. 3 (2013): 413–15.

"MCLE Requirements." State Bar of California. Accessed April 19, 2015. http://mcle.calbar.ca.gov/Attorneys/Requirements.aspx.

Otey, Brittany Stringfellow. "Millennials, Technology, and Professional Responsibility: Training a New Generation in Technological Professionalism." *Journal of the Legal Profession* 37, no. 2 (2013): 199–264.

Palfrey, John. "Cornerstones of Law Libraries for an Era of Digital-Plus." *Law Library Journal* 102, no. 2 (2010): 171–72.

Peoples, Lee F. "Designing a Law Library to Encourage Learning." *Journal of Legal Education* 63, no. 4 (2013): 612–39.

"Principles and Standards for Legal Research Competency." American Association of Law Libraries. Accessed April 19, 2015. http://www.aallnet.org/Documents/Leadership-Governance/Policies/policy-legalrescompetency.pdf.

"Private Law Libraries Special Interest Section (PLL-SIS)." American Association of Law Libraries. Accessed July 7, 2015. http://www.aallnet.org/sections/pll.

"Publications." American Association of Law Libraries Legal History & Rare Books Special Interest Section (LHRB-SIS). Available at http://www.aallnet.org/sections/lhrb/publications. Note: The LHRB-SIS quarterly newsletter and annual review are available at this site.

Rumsey, Mary. "Foreign and International Law Librarianship." *Legal Reference Services Quarterly* 25, nos. 2–3 (2006): 73–88.

Schlit, Margaret A. "Faculty Services in the 21st Century: Evolution and Innovation." *Legal Reference Services Quarterly* 26, nos. 1–2 (2007): 187–207.

"SIS [Special Interest Section] Websites." *American Association of Law Libraries.* Accessed July 7, 2015. http://www.aallnet.org/mm/Member-Communities/sis/sis-websites.

"State, Court & County Law Libraries Special Interest Section, County Public Law Library Standards: April, 2009." American Association of Law Libraries. Accessed April 19, 2015. http://www.aallnet.org/sections/sccll/docs/countystandards2009.pdf.

Stevens, Ruth S. "Legal Research: Is There an App for That?" *Michigan Bar Journal* 91, no. 6 (2012): 54–55.

Technical Services Law Librarian. American Association of Law Libraries. Accessed February 17, 2015. http://www.aallnet.org/sis/tssis/tsll/.

"Unauthorized Practice of Law Toolkit." American Association of Law Libraries State, Court & County Law Libraries Special Interest Section. Accessed April 19, 2015. http://www.aallnet.org/sections/sccll/toolkit/Unauthorized -Practice-of-Law.

University of Michigan Law School. "The Value of Law Librarians at Law Firms." *The Law Quadrangle: Notes from Michigan Law* (Spring 2011). https://www.law.umich.edu/quadrangle/spring2011/specialfeatures/Pages/ TheValueofLawLibrariansatLawFirms.aspx.

Wheeler, Ronald. "AALL Diversity Redelineated." *Law Library Journal* 106, no. 1 (2014): 135–41.

Wheeler, Ronald E. "Does WestlawNext Really Change Everything? The Implications of WestlawNext on Legal Research." *Law Library Journal* 103, no. 3 (2011): 359–77.

Whisner, Mary. "Law Librarian, J.D. or Not J.D.?" *Law Library Journal* 100, no. 1 (2008): 185–90.

8 LITERATURE AND LANGUAGES LIBRARIANSHIP

Arianne Hartsell-Gundy
Duke University

INTRODUCTION

Librarians who are subject specialists for literature and languages are usually divided by which languages and countries they work with. The title "literature librarian" (sometimes called the "English librarian" or a more general title like the "humanities librarian") often refers to the person who works with the English department. This person may also work with foreign languages, or there may be librarians who specifically serve different language and culture departments, such as a librarian who is designated to work with the Romance languages department. In the latter case, it will be beneficial to also consult the chapter in this book on area studies.

Titles and responsibilities will vary from institution to institution, but generally people in these positions collect literary criticism and fiction for the languages and countries they are assigned. They may also collect materials for studying and learning languages. They will provide library instruction for literature-related courses and will answer the questions of scholars and students who are doing research related to literature. Other tasks may include outreach to departments, working a general reference desk, helping to make purchasing decisions for journals and databases, creating subject guides, and making displays. Most of the suggestions and tips for this chapter will be relevant for all literatures and languages, but special note will be made when the advice is more specifically for English and American literature, or if it relates more to working with foreign-language materials.

INTERSECTIONS WITH OTHER DISCIPLINES

Subject specialists for literature and languages will often find that their work crosses disciplines and requires coordinating and collaborating with librarians in many different areas. In some larger academic libraries, the literature librarian may just collect for one subject area, but it is very common now for subject specialists to be responsible for more than one subject area. Common disciplines that a literature librarian might have to cover include theater, linguistics, communication, film studies, and an interdisciplinary area like women's studies. Even if one is not responsible for these areas, it may still make sense to coordinate collection development and instruction with other subject specialists who do work in those areas.

The areas that are served will also vary based on what is taught in the departments. For example, English departments often include areas like composition and rhetoric, linguistics, film studies, creative writing, folklore, journalism, technical communication, cultural studies, and more. It is also not uncommon for English faculty to have joint appointments in other related departments. Librarians who work with languages may work closely with traditional language departments, but they may also support "area studies," which will require not just knowing the language or literature of a country, but will also cross into the history, politics, and culture of that country. It may also not be as simple as supporting one country. For example, supporting French studies may extend to supporting all of the francophone countries.

In addition to covering a variety of disciplines, one's work will often cross over with various library departments and librarians who are not subject specialists, depending on the needs of the disciplines. Since the basic required first-year writing course is often situated in English departments, a literature librarian may be heavily involved in providing library instruction for basic writing courses. This may require working closely with an instruction coordinator and/or a First-Year Experience librarian to provide instruction for these students. Topics for first-year writing courses may not be focused on literature, though instructors may teach rhetorical devices and use composition theories. These departments are often heavy users of special collections, so a literature and language librarian may work closely with special collections departments to provide instruction and research support. It is also possible that a subject specialist may become involved with collection decisions for manuscripts, first editions, and rare books. Another area where a literature and languages librarian may be expected to play a role is in the growing area of digital humanities. Many libraries are beginning to expect humanities librarians to have these kinds of skills. At a minimum, this shift is reflected in the requirements and preferences listed in job ads. In some cases, job titles are changing. It is increasingly common to see titles such as "Librarian for English and Digital Humanities." It is likely that the literature and languages subject specialist will need to work closely with digital scholarship librarians and various digital centers.

WORKPLACES

Typically, a humanities subject specialist works in an academic library, though larger public libraries might employ subject specialists for collection development and research support. Also, a librarian who has a literature background could use that knowledge to provide readers' advisory at a public library. Depending on background and library coursework, a literature librarian could also work in a special collections department as a curator of literature at an academic library. Some nonprofit organizations and museums settings could benefit from this background as well, depending on their foci and their particular needs.

SPECIAL REQUIREMENTS FOR THE POSITION

A second master's degree is not required, but it can be quite valuable in understanding the subject matter and appreciating the research methods used by literary scholars. Some faculty may also treat the subject specialist with those additional credentials as more of a colleague and less of a clerk. In fact, a PhD is not unheard of for people in this role. Though people take many different paths to librarianship, a large number of library science students have a bachelor's degree in English, and the search committee for literature librarian positions will often field hundreds of applications. A second master's degree can help set someone apart from other candidates. Also, if a librarian wants to specialize in literature written in another language, a master's degree may help increase proficiency and provide proof of strong skills in that language. Time and money are of course always a concern when completing schooling, so explore different options that may be available. If still deciding on a library school, find programs that offer dual-degree options. These kinds of programs allow a student to work on both degrees at the same time. It may also be possible to pursue the second master's degree while working as a professional librarian.

Some libraries will want three to five years of experience in a professional position. If a recent graduate from a library science program is struggling to find a position as a literature and languages librarian, that person may need to spend a few years in a related position. Spending three to five years in a general position, such as working as an instruction librarian or a reference librarian, can be beneficial preparation for working as a subject specialist.

MASTER OF LIBRARY SCIENCE AND OTHER COURSEWORK

There are a couple of basic library science courses that are important for all subject specialists: reference, collection development, and instruction. If one's library science program offers a humanities reference/resources course, it is highly recommended. These courses are a good place to learn about some of the general print and electronic resources in the field, common kinds of research questions, and trends in the field. Also, these kinds of courses are often taught by practicing subject specialists, a valuable resource for learning how the job really works. Other classes that might be helpful are collection management courses, cataloging courses, technology courses, management courses, and courses that cover topics like information-seeking behavior, assessment, and usability.

Taking courses in one's library science program should be the first priority, but consider taking some electives in other departments. A course that covers digital humanities tools and theories will be especially beneficial. Some tools and skills that might be useful to learn include data visualization, text analysis, text mining, Text Encoding Initiative coding, or geographic information systems (commonly referred to as "GIS") and mapping. Though the software will change over time, becoming familiar with programs like Omeka and Wordpress will also be valuable. (Professional organizations also offer many conference programs and online courses, workshops, and webinars on digital scholarship. These are convenient options for both master of library science students and practicing librarians to learn more and keep up to date on these topics.) A history of the book course will not only be fun, but it will also provide some grounding in publishing history and theories surrounding book history. If a subject specialist chooses not to get a second master's degree, that person should at least contemplate taking a literary theory course or a research methods course in the humanities to gain some experience in how faculty conduct their research. Even if one's undergraduate degree is in English or a foreign language, an increased understanding of how research is done at the scholarly level can be useful. There may be an expectation of publishing for tenure or continuing contract at one's future institution. It's wise to consider taking a research methods in the social sciences course and a statistics course, as these provide excellent preparation for performing scholarly research. Writing a library science journal article is a much easier process if one actually understands how to collect data and process statistics, skills that people with humanities degrees often lack.

For those who want to be a subject specialist for languages, there are several different kinds of courses that should be considered. One may need to take language courses, depending on one's level of experience in that language. A librarian specializing in languages should aim for at least reading knowledge since that person will be purchasing materials for those areas. If a person is already fluent in one language, that person should think about taking courses in other languages. For instance, if someone has majored in French as an undergraduate, he or she may then decide to become a language subject specialist, but this position may require working with other Romance languages besides just French, so it would be advantageous to gain a working knowledge of Spanish while in graduate school.

In addition to language skills, a language subject specialist will also benefit from taking a few other classes. If one is a language specialist, there may be an expectation of doing original cataloging in that language, depending on the size of the institution and how rare the language is. A language specialist may also have to play a greater role in acquisitions since there will be a need to work with foreign vendors. It is quite possible that the language subject specialist will be the only person in the library with any fluency in a particular language, so he or she should consider taking courses in technical services to be able to fulfill those needs.

INTERNSHIPS AND WORK EXPERIENCE

It is absolutely essential that one get experience working in a library before going on the job market. Employers want to know that a librarian can handle basic job duties like working a reference desk, and the best way to prove that one can do that kind of work is to do it. Potential literature and language librarians should look for graduate assistant positions that will provide experience doing tasks like working a reference desk, teaching library instruction workshops, and cataloging. If possible, prospective literature and language librarians should also try to find a position working for a subject specialist while in library school. In some cases, a subject specialist might be fortunate enough to be able to employ a graduate assistant. An internship or other kind of practicum experience with a subject specialist may also be a possibility. Common tasks include helping going through catalogs for collection development, updating online subject guides, writing bibliographies, and creating online or physical displays. An internship or practicum experience may also be an opportunity to collaborate with a subject specialist on a special project.

Finally, if one does pursue a second master's degree, he or she should consider being a teaching assistant for a literature or language class. It can be a great way to understand the curriculum needs of faculty and graduate students. Plus it is a great chance to gain a lot of useful classroom experience.

CAREER PATHS

Librarians who choose to move into a management position usually have a couple of options. Depending on how the library is structured, there may be an opportunity to become the head of a group of subject specialists (the title may be something like "head of humanities group"). Another venue may be to become the head of a humanities and arts library, if the campus's library system has multiple branches. The skills a subject specialist acquires may also make one eligible to become the head of a reference department or a head/coordinator of collection development, depending on one's interests and the needs of the library.

Some librarians will advance by going through a continuing-contract process (similar to a tenure process) and will move up the ranks from assistant librarian to associate librarian and finally full librarian. Librarians who take this route will find opportunities throughout their career to take on new challenges by teaching undergraduate courses, becoming adjunct instructors in library schools, leading library and university committees, and so on. Either path is valid and can lead to a satisfying career.

PROFESSIONAL ORGANIZATIONS

Professional organizations are a great way to network with colleagues, gain leadership experience, and learn more about how to do one's job. Even seasoned subject specialists benefit from learning from colleagues. Probably the two most beneficial organizations to join are the Association of College and Research Libraries (ACRL), which is a division of the American Library Association, and the Modern Language Association (MLA). If a librarian joins ACRL, that librarian can then join relevant sections that focus on disciplines or job functions. If one is working with American and English literature, he or she will want to consider joining the ACRL Literatures in English Section (LES). Depending on languages that one works with, there are several sections that might be useful, including the Asian, African, and Middle Eastern Section (AAMES), the Slavic and East European Section (SEES), and the Western European Studies Section (WESS). These sections will provide opportunities for exchanging ideas with librarians doing similar work. There will often be relevant discussion groups and programs at conferences, social media pages, newsletters, social events, and active listservs where one can ask questions and find job advertisements. Some sections provide mentoring programs, and there are opportunities to serve on a variety of committees.

Joining the MLA will help a subject specialist keep up with the trends in literature and languages. There is a discussion group called the Libraries and Research in Languages and Literatures that meets at the MLA conference, and the ACRL LES and WESS sections sponsor a liaison to the organization. The MLA conference can be overwhelming, but it is a great way to find out about the research being done by scholars. Even if one does not go to their conferences, there is still benefit in being a member of MLA through joining some of their discussion groups and listservs and by reading their publications. MLA also has opportunities for librarians to become field bibliographers for the *Modern Language Association International Bibliography*. Field bibliographers write descriptions and bibliographical information about publications that are indexed in the *Modern Language Association International Bibliography*.

There are a variety of other organizations that one may consider joining, though additional memberships will depend greatly on one's finances, time, and interests. Sometimes it can be beneficial to join an organization to help build knowledge in areas that a librarian is not as comfortable with. For example, if theater is an area a subject specialist has to work with, and one is unfamiliar with that field, the Theater Library Association might be a very helpful organization to join. Other useful organizations might include options like the National Council of Teachers of English, the Alliance of Digital Humanities Organizations, and the Popular Culture Association. There are also many other groups under the American Library Association umbrella that may be beneficial, such as the ACRL Instruction Section, the ACRL Digital Humanities Interest Group, and the Library Instruction Round Table. Local and state associations can be an excellent way to meet one's counterparts at other libraries, which can lead to opportunities for collaboration and information sharing.

PUBLICATIONS TO FOLLOW

Though it can be hard to find the time, regular reading of scholarly and professional publications is a good way to keep up with new ideas and theories. Even sometimes skimming titles and abstracts can help one learn what scholars are discussing in their fields. Many journals allow readers to create alerts and RSS feeds to help keep up with what is being published.

Besides some ACRL section newsletters, there is not a journal devoted to literature and languages librarianship, but there may be many articles of interest in different professional library journals, such as *Reference & User Services Quarterly*, *Portal: Libraries and the Academy*, *College & Research Libraries*, *Journal of Information Literacy*, and *Collection Management*. One helpful strategy is to search within these journals, or in databases like *Library, Information Science, and Technology Abstracts (LISTA)*, for relevant keywords like "humanities," "literary research," "subject specialists," or "digital humanities."

In addition to reading library-related journals, it can be useful to read some of the scholarly journals in the field. There are several general literature journals that will be very useful, such as *PMLA*, *Year's Work in English Studies*, *Year's Work in Critical and Cultural Theory*, and *American Literature*. *PMLA* is an MLA membership perk, so it can be an especially easy journal to gain access to. Of course there are many specialized journals that one might find useful, depending on the strengths of one's collection and gaps in one's knowledge. For instance, if the English department specializes in postcolonial studies, the subject specialist for that department might want to take a look at a journal like *Postcolonial Studies*. Many of these kinds of publications provide reviews of scholarly monographs.

Since most literature librarians will collection current fiction, reading reviews is a necessary part of collection development. It is recommended that one not read just library-specific review sources such as *Booklist* and *Library Journal*, but also publications like *World Literature Today*, the *New York Times* book review section, the *New York Review of Books*, the *London Review of Books*, and *Book Forum*.

In addition to reading journals, prospective literature librarians should consider reading relevant blogs such as *In the Library with the Lead Pipe*, *Digital Humanities Now*, *dh+lib*, and *ProfHacker* (a *Chronicle of Higher Education* blog), so that one can get the most recent news in these areas.

FINAL WORDS

The traditional work of subject specialists (reference, instruction, and collection development) still has value, but the expectations and roles are beginning to change. Subject specialists are beginning to provide support in new areas like open access and digital humanities. It is very important to keep up with the trends not just in the disciplines that one is supporting but also in librarianship in general so that one is aware of the new roles that may be expected of subject specialists. Literature and languages librarians in training should get into the habit of reading relevant literature in all of these areas, and be prepared to have to keep learning new skills.

Being a subject specialist for literature and languages is very rewarding because it is a way to combine a love of literature and languages with a love of helping people. It is also a job that provides a variety of tasks and the opportunity to work with many different scholars and students.

9 AREA STUDIES LIBRARIANSHIP

Betsaida M. Reyes
University of Kansas

INTRODUCTION

As the name suggests, area studies librarians specialize in working with geographic areas of the world in a variety of ways. The region that an area studies librarian specializes in could be a country such as Japan or a continent such as Africa.

As the world becomes more interconnected, the work of an area studies librarian increases in importance. The expertise and knowledge (generally including both deep familiarity with the region as well as skill in one or more foreign languages) are highly desirable qualities for academic libraries across the nation. Thus, area studies librarians have many opportunities open to them.

From a practical perspective, being an area studies librarian means that every day will be different given the diversity of duties. Besides managing and developing the library's collection, area studies librarians teach information literacy courses, answer research questions both at the reference desk and by e-mail, phone, instant messenger, and other media, work on special projects, and conduct research. They also get the chance to develop a close relationship with the departments they serve. Robbins (2010) explains with numbers the current trends and future needs of area studies librarians. Those changes make a career in area studies librarianship an exciting one as academic libraries move to stay a step ahead of the information needs of users of their collections.

INTERSECTIONS WITH OTHER DISCIPLINES

When one looks at the various titles of area studies librarians, it is not quite discernible what their duties encompass. Take for instance the title of a librarian at the University of Kansas: Slavic and Near East Studies Librarian. Unlike a biology subject specialist, where it is very clear that the person is responsible for library's biology collection, in the case of area studies, one can be responsible for a variety of disciplines (such as languages, history, and politics) that are linked to a specific part of the world. The aforementioned Slavic and Near East Studies Librarian has a remarkable talent for language (11 languages at the advanced level; 5 at the intermediate level; and 9 at the basic level) and has many responsibilities. He performs collection development for the Balkan Peninsula, the Near East, and linguistics. Due to his language skills, he is also the cataloger for the materials related to those regions. Though it is not the norm for subject specialists to also be catalogers, it serves as an example of how varied area studies librarians' work can be. More commonly, area studies librarians serve as reference librarians or provide library instruction.

Area studies librarians (also called "area studies bibliographers," "librarians for [name of a region of the world] studies," or sometimes simply classified as a "humanities librarian") can work with a wide range of disciplines, from history to economics to literature and everything in between. Unlike other subject specialist librarians, however, they will be responsible only for covering these disciplines as relating to their region of the world: for example, the history, economics, and language of Japan. This can get complex when materials discuss more than one area of the world. An example of this could be a book on the economic relationship between Latin America and China. If the book were written in Spanish, then it is likely that the area studies librarian responsible for Latin America would be asked to purchase it. Very expensive items that discuss multiple regions of the world may end up being funded by multiple librarians.

WORKPLACES

Most area studies librarians work in academic libraries, although a few work in large public libraries or specialized libraries. The specificity of their responsibilities varies with the size of the library. The bigger the collection size, the more specific the librarian's duties are likely to be. For example, in a small liberal arts college, the librarian who covers humanities, social sciences disciplines, and fine arts may also cover area studies if he or she has expertise on a specific region. On the other hand, in a large institution, they may cover only a particular geographic area. At the University of Kansas where the author works, there is a Librarian for African and Global and International Studies; a Librarian for Slavic Studies; an East Asian Studies Librarian; a Japanese Studies Librarian; and a Librarian for Spanish, Portuguese, Latin American and Caribbean Studies. This demonstrates that in some cases the region of the world an individual covers can be rather small, as in the case of the Japanese Studies Librarian, or rather large, as with the African and Global and International Studies Librarian. How regions are divided and assigned depends on various factors. The institution may seek a librarian with certain language skills that match the current research and curricular needs of the teaching faculty or they may seek a librarian with language skills to match that of historically divided geographical regions. In the case of the area covered by the Librarian for Spanish, Portuguese, Latin American and Caribbean Studies, one could wonder how two European countries are mixed in with most countries in another continent. The answer has to do with colonialism. Both Spain and Portugal had colonies in the New World—thus merging all of those countries under the responsibility of one area studies librarian. Keep in mind that budgets do not necessarily match the size of the area covered. Many area studies librarians may also share duties outside of their main units. They can have responsibilities to help staff the general reference desk or to work half-time as instruction librarians. They may also be responsible for performing original cataloging, especially if they are knowledgeable about several languages. The number of hours spent performing work outside of area studies varies by institution.

SPECIAL REQUIREMENTS FOR THE POSITION

Besides having a master's degree in library science (MLS), a prospective area studies librarian would usually have a second master's degree or a PhD related to the geographic area in which they want to specialize. This allows for some flexibility. Degrees may be in the social sciences, humanities, or foreign languages. The author's training is in Hispanic literature and Spanish linguistics rather than history or Latin American studies. Many librarians actually complete this "second master's degree" or PhD *before* they decide to pursue careers as librarians. Some schools offer dual master's degree programs in information science and a content area. For example, the University of Texas at Austin offers a combined master of science in information studies and master of arts in Latin American studies. Although the content area degree is often seen in the "preferred" list of qualifications rather than the "required" list, students interested in this particular line of work should regard an advanced degree in a content area almost as required since it is a defining component when evaluating the applications during the hiring process. After all, subject specialists work closely with faculty from the various departments they serve. Knowledge of their research content only helps facilitate the conversation, and thus strengthen the relationship. Librarians with additional advanced degrees may find that the research skills, content knowledge, and academic interests they bring with them also aid their work toward tenure and promotion.

Proficiency in a second language is another major component in being an area studies librarian. For many area studies positions, knowledge of one or more relevant languages may be a deciding factor in getting the position. Native speakers of a language may have an advantage in the job hunt. For example, a native Spanish speaker who grew up in Latin America has not only the language background but also knowledge of the culture. No matter what their degrees are in, they may likely be familiar with the various political issues and overall history of the area based on their years living in the region. Non-native speakers of Spanish, however, can certainly build up similar expertise through coursework and travel. These experiences would also provide the person with valuable knowledge about the country or region with which they want to work.

For both native and non-native speakers, having the experience of living in a particular country for an extended period of time provides many other valuable skills. It can give the person general information regarding, for example, the cost and availability of books. This information is very useful when dealing with vendors on either approval plans or firm orders. Having that firsthand knowledge will give the applicant an edge on the job market. For both native and non-native speakers, visiting countries in their area of interest is a great way to make a potential area studies librarian more competent.

MASTER OF LIBRARY SCIENCE AND OTHER COURSEWORK

Many information science programs offer at least one course on collection development. This type of class provides a general background in the overarching issues and concepts particular to collection development. The theories and models taught in these classes will help a librarian discuss day-to-day responsibilities related to managing a library's collection with colleagues. However, in the case of area studies librarians, the knowledge and skills necessary in collection development may come mostly from internships with another area studies librarian or through discussion lists pertaining to their area of interest. The reason for this is that most classes focus on the North American market.

It is important to take at least one course each in cataloging, archives and manuscripts, reference, and information literacy instruction. Having a basic knowledge of cataloging can make performing complicated searches in the catalog easier, and will also help when the area studies librarian is called upon to catalog non-English materials. Most area studies librarians have to provide individual research consultations or work a few hours per week at the reference desk. A course in reference will prepare them to tackle questions from faculty and students without fear. The demand for information literacy instruction has increased as holdings of electronic materials have increased, making it even more necessary to help students navigate the multitude of resources available. Area studies librarians teach students how to interact with the resources available at their institutions and beyond. Taking a course on library instruction helps librarians begin to teach with confidence. Having said that, it is important to recognize that MLS coursework tends to provide a theoretical background for instruction rather than hands-on practice. The most useful knowledge comes through actual teaching in a library.

INTERNSHIPS AND WORK EXPERIENCE

Many MLS programs offer internship opportunities so that their students may gain practical skills. Though some library science programs require a single semester-long internship to satisfy the requirements to graduate, the author advises anyone desiring a career in area studies librarianship to do more than this. A prospective area studies librarian might take part in an extended internship spanning more than one semester or complete one or two internships in different departments. They may also find part-time jobs or volunteer work in libraries that provide valuable experience. Some of these internships or other positions may not relate directly to area studies. For example, a prospective area studies librarian might choose to work in a reference or instruction department to build his or her skills in these areas.

Part-time jobs and internships will provide a prospective librarian with knowledge and skills not covered in the classroom. For example, one could be involved in a digital scholarship project related to area studies. Keep in mind that it is always advisable to intern, volunteer, or work in a similar institution where one wants to work. This means that if the ideal job is to be an academic area studies librarian, it would be preferable to gain experience in an academic library setting.

It is important to look frequently at current ads for professional positions, even if one has many semesters left before graduating. This will help prospective area studies librarians keep apprised of current trends in job requirements. This information can be used to gain the necessary experience to qualify for jobs to which they would eventually hope to apply. For example, an MLS student might notice that many positions that appeal to him requires cataloging experience. If he became aware of this while he still had time left in library school, he would have the chance to take additional cataloging courses or pursue an internship in cataloging. This would increase his chances of securing a similar job in the future.

For students interning or working part-time in collection development, attending an international book fair could provide additional practical knowledge since MLS coursework tends to focus on the North American market. For example, the Feria Internacional del Libro in Guadalajara, Mexico, is the biggest and most important book fair in Latin America. The American Library Association and the Feria Internacional del Libro have a partnership to help librarians cover some of the costs of the trip. For more information on the ALA-FIL FREE PASS Program, visit this site http://www.ala.org/offices/iro/awardsactivities/guadalajarabook.

The LéaLA—Feria del Libro en Español de Los Angeles is an alternative to further expand one's skills and knowledge in collection development without leaving the country.

Though there is no bulletproof way to secure a position as an area studies librarian, all of the strategies discussed in the paragraphs above make one's curriculum vitae stand out.

CAREER PATHS

For some librarians, moving up in the ranks is the way to go. They find that they work best when they can continue to work on the collections for their areas and have that continuous connection with the departments for which they are liaisons. Many others find that they are interested in leadership opportunities.

They can become heads of area studies units or even heads of collection development departments. Some area studies librarians stay in the same institution for decades while others choose to move from one institution to the next as positions become available. It is also possible for some librarians with deeper knowledge of a subject to also become a teaching faculty member in their academic departments, thus receiving joint appointments as professors.

Some area studies librarians find employment outside of academic libraries. Museums, large public libraries, and cultural heritage organizations often hire those with expertise in both librarianship and languages. Publishers, including those that create databases, as well as book vendors frequently hire area studies librarians to help design and sell products in multiple languages for libraries.

PROFESSIONAL ORGANIZATIONS

There are many professional organizations one can join to stay abreast of the developments in area studies based on the geographical area of interest. The following list is meant to provide a general overview of organizations dedicated to major regions of area studies. The list is not comprehensive. It is important to keep in mind that some organizations are ideal to join as students because they will provide you with valuable information. Once new librarians begin their careers, there will be other organizations that will be relevant to their position.

Latin American Studies

Seminar on the Acquisition of Latin American Library Materials http:// salalm.org/

Founded in 1956, it has provided the only national and international forum focused on Latin American studies for academic and research library collections and services. The Seminar on the Acquisition of Latin American Library Materials offers special student rates, and it is highly advisable that students join and attend conferences before graduating. Doing so will provide students with access to a community of librarians, academics, and others interested in Latin American studies librarianship. Through an e-mail list, members can learn about issues, resources, new opportunities, and open positions. There are several scholarship opportunities available to help its new members (especially students) attend the annual meetings and to encourage involvement. The organization provides new members with the option of joining a mentorship program, as well as committees that align with their interest.

Western European Studies

The Association of College and Research Libraries' (ACRL) Western European Studies Section *(WESS) http://www.ala.org/acrl/aboutacrl/ directoryofleadership/sections/wess/acr-wesec*

WESS promotes the improvement of library services supporting study and research in western European affairs from ancient times to the present.

Slavic Studies

Midwest Slavic and Eurasian Library Consortium https://midslav.wordpress .com/

The Midwest Slavic and Eurasian Library Consortium promotes cooperation among member libraries in support of Slavic and Eurasian studies throughout the United States and Canada. Originally founded in 1996 as the Kansas Slavic Consortium, the group currently consists of seven member libraries primarily from the midwestern United States.

Pacific Coast Slavic and East European Library Consortium http://intranet .library.arizona.edu/users/brewerm/pacslav/

The group was formed to promote the development of Slavic studies resources in the Pacific region of the United States and Canada.

East Coast Consortium of Slavic Library Collections http://www.eccslavic.org/

Established in 1993, the East Coast Consortium helps coordinate the activities of Eurasian area studies library collections located in the eastern United States and Canada.

Asian Studies

Council on East Asian Libraries http://www.eastasianlib.org/

The Council on East Asian Libraries was founded in 1958 as the Committee on American Library Resources on the Far East and built on earlier organizations going back to 1948. As a nonprofit organization, the Council on East Asian Libraries' mission is to serve as a forum for the discussion of East Asian library issues of common concern; to formulate programs for the development of East Asian library resources, services, and systematic organization of all types of recorded information and knowledge; and to promote interlibrary and international cooperation in East Asian librarianship. *Note:* Librarians must be members of the Association for Asian Studies in order to join the Council on East Asian Libraries.

North American Coordinating Council on Japanese Library Resources http://guides.nccjapan.org/homepage

Founded in 1991, the North American Coordinating Council on Japanese Library Resources works closely with librarians, faculty, and funding agencies to strengthen Japanese-language collections and to promote access to information in all forms and formats. The North American Coordinating Council collaborates closely with Japanese institutions, leading organizations in North America, and other global institutions with interests in Japanese studies to develop consortial relationships, as well as to create and disseminate services.

Society for Chinese Studies Librarians http://www.scsl-web.org/

Established in March 2010 in the United States, the Society for Chinese Studies Librarians is a nonprofit, nonpolitical academic organization aimed at promoting scholarly activities, professional exchange, information sharing, and project cooperation among Chinese studies librarians, so as to make contributions to China studies in general and to Chinese resources study in particular.

Asian Pacific American Librarians Association (APALA) http://www .apalaweb.org/

A predecessor of APALA, the Asian American Librarians Caucus (AALC) was organized in 1975 as a discussion group of the American Library Association Office for Library Outreach Services reflecting the interest in library services to minority communities and professional support of librarians of minority ancestry during the 1960s and 1970s. APALA officially became affiliated with the American Library Association in 1982. In 2014–15, APALA became part of the Joint Council of Librarians of Color, along with American Indian Library Association, Black Caucus of the American Library Association, Chinese American Librarians Association, and REFORMA.

African Studies

Africana Librarians Council http://www.library.upenn.edu/collections/ africa/ALC/

The Africana Librarians Council was founded in 1957 as part of the African Studies Association under the name Archives/Libraries Committee. The Africana Librarians Council continues today as a coordinate organization of the African Studies Association. Members of the African Studies Association, including librarians, scholars, archivists, and documentary filmmakers, research and preserve materials from and about Africa. *Note:* Librarians must be members of the African Studies Association in order to join the Africana Librarians Council.

PUBLICATIONS TO FOLLOW

Prospective area studies librarians may want to follow publications from the field of library science as well as content area journals written for academic faculty and others with interests in a particular region of the world. Interestingly, content area journals often publish library-themed articles. For example, Latin American studies librarians can publish their work on the *Latin American Research Review*, a journal put out by the Latin American Studies Association.

Library science journals that prospective area studies librarians may want to follow include:

- *Collection Building*, a journal dedicated to all aspects of library collection development and maintenance from the practical to the theoretical
- *Collection Management*, an essential refereed quarterly journal that presents practical, research-based information about building, administering, preserving, assessing, and organizing library collections
- *Library Resources and Technical Services*, a peer-reviewed journal that takes a critical approach to the questions and challenges facing librarians and libraries. Major topics include collection development, scholarly communication, preservation (including digitization), acquisitions (including licensing and economic aspects of acquisitions), continuing resources, and cataloging (including descriptive metadata, authority control, subject analysis, and classification).

FINAL WORDS

Area studies librarianship is an attractive career due to the flexibility it provides. It gives librarians the chance to teach, stay in touch with the trends in their field of interest, conduct research, and travel. There are unique opportunities to learn more about the culture and research output in those countries. It can also be a chance to establish and build relationships between institutions that are mutually beneficial.

Though books and other materials are important resources when gathering information on what career to choose, the advice of an experienced area studies professional can help in navigating the specifics of their area. A good mentor can improve the experience as a student and can serve as a support system as the student progresses in his or her career.

REFERENCE

Robbins, Louise. "Subject Specialists for Academic and Research Libraries: Research, Recruitment and Education." (2010). Retrieved from http://slisweb.lis.wisc.edu/~imls/findings%282%29.htm.

10 GOVERNMENT INFORMATION LIBRARIANSHIP

Shari Laster
University of California, Santa Barbara

INTRODUCTION

Government information librarians, also known as "government documents librarians" or simply "docs librarians," are experts in the official content created and disseminated by governmental entities. They build and manage government documents collections in a variety of formats, respond to basic reference questions and complex research inquiries related to governments and their information products, teach library users and librarians about government information resources, create and update accurate descriptions of government publications, and advocate for access to and preservation of these materials.

Whether in a full- or part-time assignment, a government information librarian is responsible for making content from government sources available to the library's users and the surrounding community. In the United States, this is most frequently information from the federal government and the government of the state in which the library is located. Some libraries also collect resources from foreign, state or provincial, and local governmental entities, and many build collections that include materials from international governmental organizations such as the United Nations, European Union, or World Bank; as well as materials from nongovernmental organizations like think tanks and nonprofits.

In the United States, federal government documents have expanded in scope and reach from the first century of the country's history. Core collections of government publications typically include bills and laws, documentation of congressional debates and votes, presidential directives and communications with Congress, federal court opinions, and a wide array of reports, documents, maps, and other materials from agencies and other bodies commissioned to carry out the law as set forth by Congress. More recent government documents communicate with U.S. residents and citizens about their rights, opportunities, and responsibilities. Government information also includes data and statistical resources, promotional and educational media, reports disseminating the results of federally funded research, websites and social media, and much more. Virtually every topic that is a potential subject for legislation is addressed in a government information product somewhere.

Historically, libraries have collected and organized government information based on provenance (in this case, the government organization that created it) rather than content. Consequently, while many librarians are competent in accessing and managing basic government resources, having a specialist on staff is helpful and frequently necessary in addressing research needs and managing research-level collections and resources. Docs librarians also manage their library's participation in public documents distribution programs. Within the United States, federal government information resources are distributed to libraries via the Federal Depository Library Program (FDLP), which is managed by the U.S. Government Publishing Office (GPO). In addition to administering the FDLP, GPO publishes core federal documents titles in print and digital formats; catalogs and indexes federal publications; and collects digital government publications from federal agencies.

INTERSECTIONS WITH OTHER DISCIPLINES

By the very nature of governance, government information engages with virtually every aspect of everyday life. While government information librarians most commonly support the work of social sciences librarians, they also collaborate on a regular basis with general reference, applied sciences, humanities, law, business, and area studies librarians. Conversely, librarians in those specialties benefit from familiarity with government information resources.

Many government information librarians work in public services roles, particularly reference, instruction, and collection management; however, other docs librarians serve in technical services roles. Government documents present specific challenges with respect to cataloging and metadata, and librarians managing large collections benefit from developing extended collaborations with cataloging, metadata, and systems librarians. Docs librarians also routinely address access, reference, research, and collection management issues, regardless of their work environment. Many government information librarians work collaboratively at consortial and national levels to address systemic issues related to the management of these resources.

A sizable portion of geospatial resources collected by libraries, including maps and spatial data, is produced by government entities, and consequently government information librarians have a long tradition of managing maps collections or collaborating with maps librarians. Similarly, because the government is the primary disseminator of demographic and economic data within the United States, government information librarians have provided support for access to statistical data products for decades. As more libraries turn to hiring professionals specializing in geographic information systems (usually referred to as "GIS") and data resources, docs librarians can use their expertise in the creation, dissemination, and usage of these resources to collaborate with their colleagues.

With the shift to primarily web-based distribution, documents that may have previously resided on library shelves throughout the United States are now appearing on (and sometimes disappearing from) government websites. The library community has long recognized the need for collecting and managing born-digital content, and at this time a patchwork of institutions and consortia are working to collect and preserve a portion of the enormous and rapidly growing digital content produced by government entities. Consequently, web-archiving specialists are increasingly part of the broader community of government information librarians, as are librarians engaging in digitization and digital preservation efforts.

A small but growing contingent of government information librarians focus on providing e-government services. These librarians support the long-standing role of public libraries in connecting their users with essential services. The digital divide continues to create an environment in which some individuals struggle to complete tasks that were previously conducted by mail or phone but now require the use of a computer and at least a basic level of comfort in navigating government websites and electronic forms. While nearly every docs librarian has been called upon to locate forms and assist users in navigating government websites and services, e-government specialists also work to identify and reduce barriers to access for vital services.

WORKPLACES

Government information librarians provide services and support needed in general academic libraries, community college and tribal college libraries, public libraries, academic law libraries, court libraries, and state and federal libraries. Libraries are more likely to have a government information librarian on staff if they are a member of a depository program, although notable exceptions include law firm libraries and county law libraries. The majority of libraries participating in the FDLP are academic libraries, ranging from community colleges, to liberal arts and teaching colleges, to some of the largest public and private research universities in the United States. (An interactive map of FDLP libraries by state is available at http://www.fdlp.gov/about-the-fdlp/federal-depository-libraries.) A majority of government information specialists work at academic libraries, frequently but by no means exclusively at mid- to large-size public research universities.

SPECIAL REQUIREMENTS FOR THE POSITION

There are no special requirements for becoming a government information librarian, and there is no typical academic background for librarians entering the specialization. Some interest in politics or economics is desirable, as information requests can track recent events, but no additional degree or course of study is required. Similarly, while a broad range of technical skills is an asset in navigating the changing world of accessing and preserving these resources, it is not typically a requirement for positions. New librarians are an asset to the specialization, particularly when they have the time, enthusiasm, and institutional support to unravel long-standing problems in work flows and promote underutilized collections. More broadly, a desire to support the goal of providing permanent no-fee public access to government information is essential in motivating docs librarians to advocate for these collections to their users, colleagues, and administrations.

MASTER OF LIBRARY SCIENCE AND OTHER COURSEWORK

There is a long-standing recognition of the need for public services librarians from all disciplines to become familiar with government information. A number of library and information science programs offer a government information course, frequently taught by a practitioner. These courses are usually a survey of government information resources, although some take the additional step of exploring challenges to long-term access to these materials. Master of library science courses and workshops do not typically cover depository management in depth, but they provide a solid background for government information reference and research support.

Future government information librarians also benefit from coursework in legal information, business and statistical information, cataloging and metadata, digital collections, digitization, geographic information systems, instruction, and outreach. Because of the diversity in content, format, and intended audiences for government information resources, librarians working with government information should expect to continue developing new and broader skillsets throughout their careers.

While the Federal Depository Library Conference has been a hub for educational opportunities over the past decades, in recent years GPO has also drastically expanded the number of webinars and virtual training sessions related to government information resources and services. These FDLP Academy webinars are open to the public and available for later viewing at no charge. GPO also conducts virtual training for new depository coordinators on a regular basis. Some professional organizations also offer virtual sessions on government information topics; in particular, the North Carolina Library Association's Government Resources Section is a leader in presenting educational webinars, and makes its recordings available for later viewing.

INTERNSHIPS AND WORK EXPERIENCE

The best experience to prepare for a position as a government information librarian is to work for an established government information librarian. Processing incoming materials provides familiarity with the content and conventions that are typical of tangible documents collections, and can also serve as an introduction to integrated library systems. Shadowing librarians as they respond to government information reference questions and provide library instruction provides firsthand insight into how these resources are used at the institution. Processing withdrawn materials can directly demonstrate the ways in which government information librarians are being asked to balance access and preservation concerns with the library's space considerations. Finally, working with a docs librarian is an opportunity to learn directly about the specialization, and to take the first steps in understanding the history of government documents in library collections.

A position at a law library, state library, or historical society can provide an opportunity to work with government documents collections, and may offer the chance to work with materials that present similar challenges. In addition to identifying opportunities to work directly with government documents, those who are new to the specialization can also seek out mentors, as the cadre of docs librarians who are professionally active at the national level includes practitioners with decades of expertise. Many of these practitioners are enthusiastic about providing mentorship to the next generation of docs librarians.

Both content and information dissemination trends are changing rapidly with the advent of new technologies. Some federal agencies and federal libraries offer internships that provide hands-on experience addressing new projects and programs. These internships are posted on USAJOBS (https://www.usajobs.gov) along with federal employment opportunities, and similar resources may exist at the state level.

CAREER PATHS

By virtue of working with library resources that fall outside the typical monograph and serials acquisition, management, and deaccessioning work flows, government information librarians have the opportunity to develop areas of expertise that extend beyond the traditional portfolio of public services librarians. Successful practitioners are able to build connections among library staff with differing responsibilities and priorities in order to actively manage collections and collaborate on cross-functional projects. These are skills that lead some docs librarians to choose to move into careers typically associated with library administration.

Although not a common career path, some government information librarians move from academic or law libraries to federal or state libraries and archives throughout the course of their careers. Working with government documents gives librarians expertise in the systems that produce these information products, which is valuable expertise for the civil servants charged with managing these collections on behalf of agencies.

PROFESSIONAL ORGANIZATIONS

The Government Documents Round Table (GODORT) of the American Library Association is a focused community for all aspects of government information librarianship. GODORT committees and task forces host programs and meetings that educate participants on current obstacles to locating, using, and maintaining resources from all levels of government. Members of GODORT also build tools and resources to solve problems related to providing research support and managing government information collections. Within the American Library Association, GODORT is recognized as a voice of expertise on policy and administrative issues affecting short- and long-term access to government information materials.

Other American Library Association organizations that engage with government information on a regular basis are the Map & Geospatial Information Round Table (MAGIRT) and the Federal & Armed Forces Libraries Round Table (FAFLRT). Within the Association of College and Research Libraries (ACRL), the Law and Political Science Section (LPSS) and the Numeric and Geospatial Data Services in Academic Libraries Interest Group (DIG) are additional venues for discussing these resources.

Similarly, the Government Documents Special Interest Section of the American Association of Law Libraries is a dedicated advocate for access to and preservation of legal resources from all levels of government, including legislation, court opinions, and congressional publications. The Special Libraries Association has a Government Information Division, which focuses on government library service.

Some state-level library associations have sections focused on government documents, while other states have independent councils or round tables. These organizations serve in part as state-level implementation groups for issues related to federal documents, and they give government information librarians access to a wealth of experience for state-specific resources. New government information librarians will almost invariably benefit from contacting their state's assigned FDLP Regional Depository librarian and inquiring about professional meetings. These smaller groups also provide an excellent opportunity to network within a state and serve as an active member of a professional organization.

Regardless of career path, government information librarians gain enormous benefits from proactively networking, both virtually and face-to-face. In many cases, a docs librarian is the only specialist or expert for these resources within an institution, and both problem-solving and professional growth and collaboration opportunities come from outside the institution and even outside formal structures and relationships. The opportunity to build fruitful connections within a state and at the national level is one of the most rewarding aspects of government information librarianship.

PUBLICATIONS TO FOLLOW

GODORT's professional journal *DttP: Documents to the People* is published quarterly and is available via open access following a one-year embargo. The articles are typically written by government information librarians, with one annual issue dedicated to papers by library and information science students on government information topics. *Government Information Quarterly*, published by Elsevier, focuses on policy and information technology issues affecting the creation, distribution, and usage of governmental resources around the world.

GPO produces an e-mail newsletter called *FDLP Connection* that is published on a bimonthly basis as of this writing. The *Connection* provides updates on GPO's operations and governance, and highlights government documents collections and services at libraries across the country. The *Connection* is also an important source of communication from the Depository Library Council, which is the advisory committee to the director of the GPO and the superintendent of documents.

Although mostly unaffiliated with professional organizations, government documents listservs are a vital component in keeping up to date with the profession. The GOVDOC-l listserv addresses all aspects of government documents, including depository collection management, research queries, advice and support, and discussion of current events. DOCTECH-l focuses on technical aspects of processing federal documents, while INTL-DOC addresses issues specific to the collection and management of materials from international governmental organizations, nongovernmental organizations, and foreign governments. Most states also have a government documents listserv to provide updates and share information.

FINAL WORDS

Over the past several decades, government information librarianship has reinvented itself as librarians navigate the changing models of government information distribution in the face of new and challenging landscapes for library collections and services. In the United States, the national landscape for federal government information has transitioned to a disaggregated distribution model in which agencies publish materials on websites, and reorganize or remove materials as their immediate needs require. The work of GPO and libraries in collecting these materials has shifted from a model in which resources were captured and distributed to libraries for public use, to an overabundance of rapidly decaying and difficult-to-discover digital resources in an environment in which the user discovery process frequently bypasses libraries entirely.

In an era in which physical space is at a premium and library collection size is no longer viewed as an independent arbiter of quality, librarians managing collections of tangible materials are often asked to justify their usage of the library's limited physical space, or are tasked with the responsibility of reducing the footprint of the physical collection while continuing to meet the needs of local users, the surrounding community, and consortial or statewide lending obligations. To the extent possible, these projects require a knowledgeable approach and careful hand to ensure that decisions are made responsibly. Similarly, decisions to reduce or eliminate physical collections in favor of digital collections that are not hosted or managed by the library present serious issues to long-term access, and need to be evaluated with an eye toward the long-term role of the library within its institution.

The shrinking national collection places the FDLP and similar programs at a critical juncture, where there is now a real danger that taxpayer-funded resources may no longer be available for use in the formats in which they are needed. Practitioners are needed to join the national conversation on long-term access and preservation strategies, and to reconsider collection strategies for emerging formats. Motivated librarians are also needed to implement new work flows that may include locating "lost" documents to submit to depository programs and accepting digital deposits of government information.

As library administrators continue to move toward hiring generalist positions that require less expertise in any given area, they provide fewer opportunities for specialized expertise to grow and develop. With fewer government information specialists out in the field, knowledge of government information resources is integral to more areas of librarianship, even as the national pool of experience is diminished by promotions and retirements.

Still, government information librarians are filling critical roles as multidisciplinary content specialists and cross-functional work flow specialists, even as they continue to collaboratively manage the official informational output of governments. Pressures on libraries to grow and evolve lead to new opportunities and an increased understanding of the critical importance of articulating the relationship between the institutional mission and the role of the library in serving its users now and into the foreseeable future. Docs librarians also have the opportunity to tie their work to the strategic role of their libraries within their own institutions. While the overall picture remains uncertain for permanent no-fee public access to all government information resources, it is clear that government information librarians are best positioned to take up the challenge and work toward a future of government information for all.

REFERENCES

"Federal Depository Libraries." [Map of FDLP libraries by state.] Federal Depository Library Program. Accessed August 25, 2015. http://www.fdlp.gov/about-the-fdlp/federal-depository-libraries.
"USAJOBS." U.S. Office of Personnel Management. Accessed July 15, 2015. https://www.usajobs.gov.

11 EDUCATION, PSYCHOLOGY, SOCIOLOGY, AND SOCIAL WORK LIBRARIANSHIP

Lise M. Dyckman
former Library Director, California Institute
of Integral Studies

Laura Koltutsky
University of Calgary

INTRODUCTION

While education, psychology, social work, and sociology are not the only behavioral or social science disciplines found in college and university settings (economics, politics, international affairs, and sometimes communications and journalism are also included under that umbrella), in many ways they form the core of what's considered a social science as opposed to a pure or hard science, or an art. Starting from broad generalities, it's accurate to say that social sciences are primarily concerned with human behavior; acknowledge that humans interact in societies (which have their own dynamics); and strive to objectively study individual human and collective social reality (to the extent that objectivity can be possible). Within that over-general definition, the disciplines of education, psychology, sociology and social work each have their own distinct (but overlapping) spheres. Psychology is the study of individual minds (ideas and emotions), whereas education is concerned with the cognitive development (learning) of individuals over time; sociology the study of groups of people in relationship to each other; and social work is concerned with maximizing collective well-being across different social groups. They all presume that we have normative patterns—of learning, of mental health, of social well-being, of optimal development—that reflect idealized social values and worldviews.

Social sciences are often thought of as somewhere in between the polar opposites of pure science and humanities. There is some truth to that view—but like all such schemes, rigid categories fall apart when closely examined.

That's a high-level view of these disciplines. Bringing the discussion down to a more practical level, it's useful to note that scholars in these fields tend to work in similar ways. They communicate professionally with each other primarily through journal articles, conferences (and conference proceedings), and books; and informally through blogs and online discussions. Their patterns of scholarly publication are not noticeably different from other disciplines, but there are some finer distinctions. For example, important subgenres for articles are case studies, case reports, descriptions and analyses of programs (in addition to that perennial favorite, the "review of the literature"); and these can be as influential as experiments conducted according to accepted scientific methods. Also, unlike some of the "harder" sciences, books are still important resources, especially when used to introduce new theories, new models, and innovative practices into the canon. Perhaps more so than in the humanities, social scientists tend to work in partnerships with coauthors (but social scientists rarely work out of research laboratories, and so tend to have fewer coauthors than in the health sciences literature). Authors gain prestige through the usual academic pathways—doctoral degrees, teaching in prestigious universities, citations to their written works, and so on—but also a significant number of influential authors are active practitioners in their fields, working outside of academia. (Curiously, many theories and techniques used in these fields are strongly associated with their authors, e.g., Freudian theories, Jungian archetypes, Eriksonian stages of development, Maslow's hierarchy of needs, Montessori, Piaget, Freire, and others.)

KEY RESOURCES

Because so much of social science research stands on the metaphorical shoulders of prior researchers, subject specialists supporting these disciplines need to be adept at using their key bibliographic databases. Each has one primary—preeminent, even—resource: Education Resources Information Center (ERIC) for education; the American Psychological Association's (APA) PsycINFO family of databases for psychology; Sociological Abstracts (now owned by Cambridge Scientific Abstracts); and the National Association of Social Workers' Press's Social Work Abstracts. In reality, there is a significant overlap of research interests between these fields, and searchers are likely to find relevant material on topics of interest in more than one of these databases, so it is wise for librarians supporting these disciplines to be familiar with all of them. These key resources are fairly old, as online databases go (ERIC dates back to 1966; PsycINFO contains bibliographic records for publications in the second half of the nineteenth century; and Sociological Abstracts includes materials from the 1950s), and rich with a variety of publication types. However, for the most part, they do not supply full-text documents, so a significant part of subject specialists' instruction and outreach work will involve explaining the interconnected systems libraries use to provide access to texts. Also, since these resources were created by professional associations in their fields (or in ERIC's case, the U.S. Department of Education), they include built-in tools designed for practitioners to use in refining searches. Unlike the more modern approach of Google-like keyword-only searching, using these resources effectively requires understanding their idiosyncratic structure and subject terminologies. Being able to navigate professional jargon terms is especially important, since each resource has its own fairly elaborate thesaurus and hierarchical indexing practices—and it will be well worth the time spent to learn how similar terms are used differently in each of these related databases. These aren't the only useful resources, of course, and several others are listed below in the Publications to Follow section, but they are the essential ones for subject specialists in these fields to be conversant with.

RESEARCH METHODOLOGIES

Another aspect of the social sciences being considered as in between arts and humanities on one side, "harder" sciences on the other, is that they pull research methods from both, along with devising methodologies unique to these fields. In other words, a significant portion of subject specialists' work in these areas involves knowing the main research methods used by their faculty and taught in classes in their departments, and being able to assist students in grappling with surveys, tests and measurements, and the whole gamut of quantitative and qualitative research methods. (Liaison librarians can have some advantages here, since these are many of the same methodologies used to study librarianship and information science.)

Depending on how deeply students in their departments get into research, subject specialists may find themselves needing to collect test kits and (mostly psychological) measurements. These often have restrictions on who can use them, and may require supervision or special circulation policies. Even if students don't use premade test instruments in their coursework, subject specialist librarians should also be able to help researchers find appropriate tests, instruments, surveys, and so forth to use in their own work. An excellent key resource for all types of social science methodologies is Sage Research Methods Online. Also, resources like *Tests in Print*, *Mental Measurement Yearbook*, and their online counterparts are useful for identifying specialized surveys and questionnaires, as is being able to search by specific test or research method in the key databases mentioned above. Students may also use statistical software like SPSS for their coursework (and libraries may need to load that software in their computer labs and provide user support). In programs at the doctoral level, librarians may become involved with archiving and curating research data sets.

PROFESSIONAL CREDENTIALING

Nearly all colleges and universities will offer undergraduate-level overview courses in education, psychology, and sociology, but one of the important aspects of these disciplines is that in order to work as a teacher, psychologist, therapist, or social worker, both graduate-level professional education and formal professional certification or licensure are required. Syllabi, required courses, and curricula in graduate programs in these fields are usually based on the knowledge required to practice professionally, as determined by outside agencies. So it behooves subject specialists who are supporting departments that offer teacher certification, master of arts, PhD, PsyD, or EdD degree programs to be up to date on certification and licensure requirements, and how those may tie into accreditation for their departments (discussed below, under Workplace).

It is difficult to imagine learning how to be a practicing teacher, psychotherapist, or counselor solely from written material—and in fact, videos are increasingly important educational tools (so much so that there may be specific questions asked about access to professional video collections in credentialing master of arts programs). There are extensive video collections available for training teachers, psychotherapists, and counselors, both for purchase and on a subscription basis. Subject specialists in these fields should become familiar with the issues involved in acquiring, cataloging, and delivering audiovisual collections, especially around streaming video.

OTHER RECOMMENDATIONS FOR GETTING STARTED AS A NEW SUBJECT SPECIALIST

There is evidence that faculty feel that "subject knowledge and keeping up-to-date in one's subject field are seen as critically important attributes of an Academic Liaison Librarian" (Cooke 24). Subject librarians need to understand that faculty operate with many assumptions about librarians' subject expertise. It is up to individual librarians to display that willingness to learn about new subject areas. One of the first things that a new social sciences librarian should do is to try to meet with representatives from each of the subject areas their work covers. This may be a faculty member who has volunteered to be a liaison to the library or they may have been volunteered (if the latter, it will become evident quickly). If there is no liaison, the librarian should try to meet with the department head or even the dean. These meetings are intended to introduce the new subject specialist, but even more importantly, for the librarian to listen and learn about their departments. In these early meetings, it is important to be clear what a librarian can provide in terms of support for students and faculty. Words like "partner" and "collaborate" encourage faculty members to see librarians as peers rather than as support staff.

Another first step is to find out as much as possible about the departments or faculties themselves from talking to teaching faculty (including adjuncts), from reading descriptions of required and elective courses in the course catalog, and from reviewing syllabi and any notes or materials used in past library instruction sessions. LibGuides and other online research guides prepared by colleagues at your library, and particularly those created by colleagues at other colleges and universities, are very valuable resources for learning these fields, too.

INTERSECTIONS WITH OTHER DISCIPLINES

As alluded to above, there is significant overlap between these fields; they are concerned with the same or similar aspects of human existence, look at many of the same variables and phenomena, and use many of the same research methods. It's important, however, to be aware of how each field has its own lens on the same topic. For example, searching for information on Hispanic or Latino teens in ERIC is best done by combining the descriptor "Hispanic Americans" with the truncated descriptor term "high school" (not teens or adolescents), to obtain references to articles and studies on school environments and gang involvement. A similar search in PsycINFO is best done by using the check tag for adolescent age group (13–17), not words, and combining that with the thesaurus subject phrases "Latinos/Latinas" or "Mexican Americans" (because the former does not include the latter); this retrieves studies on family relationships, language use, prevalence of depression, etc. For Sociological Abstracts, though, the subject thesaurus terms are "high school students" or "adolescents" and—assuming that the searcher wanted to be that inclusive—the search string is "Hispanic Americans" or "Cuban Americans" or "Mexican Americans" or "Puerto Rican Americans"; this retrieves articles on immigration, on cross-cultural comparisons, and on social support or other protective factors for teens.

That said, each of these fields has significant overlap with other disciplines as well. Issues of public policy, politics, government, international relations, social justice, and law are tightly intertwined with each of them. Major issues of the day—ecological degradation, social welfare, human rights, transnational immigration and emigration, national identity, gender and sexual identity, war and political conflict—all touch on, and are touched by, these disciplines. Engineering and technology are likewise intertwined, particularly in the areas of artificial intelligence and human-machine interfaces.

So, too, are they connected to health sciences. Neurobiology, neuropsychology, and psychopharmacology have made discoveries in the last decade that radically change our understandings of how intelligence and emotion operate in humans; likewise recent research into how trauma can alter our genetic code to be transmitted through generations. When dealing with questions of mental health in the United States, the role of the American Psychiatric Association's *Diagnostic and Statistical Manual of Mental Disorders* in defining what constitutes mental illness cannot be overstated. Highly controversial, this book is used to define and diagnose types of mental dysfunctions by mental health caregivers, to determine qualification in programs to assist developmentally disabled or mentally ill, and to determine coverage for treatment by health insurance companies. (For example, tracing how earlier editions of the *Diagnostic and Statistical Manual of Mental Disorders* handled sexual identities, in comparison with the current *Diagnostic and Statistical Manual of Mental Disorders*, 5th ed. (often referred to as the "*DSM5*"), gives a snapshot of the history over the last 200 years of our attitudes toward sex and gender.)

WORKPLACES

The descriptions of working in an academic library contained in other chapters of this book, and the advice for would-be academic librarians, will all be valuable to subject specialists for education, psychology, sociology, or social work too, of course. But as touched on above, there are some differences between working as an academic library subject specialist for undergraduates versus supporting graduate-level programs in these fields. The latter requires more in-depth expertise on the subject specialist's part, especially in areas that matter more to professional teachers, therapists, psychologists, and social workers. Developing greater familiarity with research methods, actively collecting tests and instruments as appropriate for the curriculum, and performing professional-level collection development are all important to support advanced degrees in this area.

Librarians who support graduate- and professional-level programs in these fields may also be more actively involved with their accreditation. While entire colleges and universities will be accredited by one of the U.S. regional associations, individual programs that offer master of arts, EdD, or PsyD degrees may also be subject to additional accreditation or certification by a professional organization. The two largest education accreditation agencies in the field of education are the National Council for Accreditation of Teacher Education and the Teacher Education Accreditation Council; in 2013 these two accreditation programs were consolidated into subsidiaries of the Council for the Accreditation of Educator Preparation. The Council on Social Work Education and the APA serve as accrediting agencies for their respective fields. Accreditation of a degree in these programs is as important as having an master of library science from an American Library Association–accredited program, and often even more so—being able to get a job as a teacher (as opposed to a teacher's aide), to qualify to practice as social worker, or to conduct psychological evaluations may depend on having a degree from an accredited institution (and those who attended unaccredited programs may require further training or testing before being allowed to practice.) Accreditation primarily occurs in cycles of 5 to 10 years, and accreditors will include library collections and services as part of their assessment. Often the subject specialist librarian will be asked to help prepare assessment reports (including quantitative information about the collection, such as numbers of books and journals that have been added, disciplinary databases, and other related resources like video or test collections; also qualitative data on how the library supports students in the program with instruction and reference services, and in some cases on distance education services). It is usually wise for the subject specialist librarian to participate in the program accreditation process, by volunteering if necessary, to demonstrate the importance of what they do for their department(s) both internally and externally.

Larger research universities may have separate branch libraries for these disciplines, either individually or in combination (education and psychology is a common pairing, as is psychology and social work). There are also smaller schools—teachers' colleges, for example, or schools of professional psychology—that focus solely on professional education for teachers, psychologists, or psychoanalysts. Librarians working in these settings share many of the same experiences as their colleagues in a unified university library setting, but may face greater challenges (with budgets, with finding adequate staff, with space for collections) and have additional advantages (of greater contact with faculty and students, and a more visible position within the organization).

Education librarians may also work in curriculum centers that collect children's literature, kits, curriculum materials, and K–12 textbooks. These curriculum centers may exist within another library or they may be connected to an education department. Librarian subject specialists for psychology may also work in health care settings (medical centers, hospitals, and even secure psychiatric hospitals connected to correctional facilities). There are some positions for librarians with experience as social work specialists with advocacy organizations and nongovernmental organizations.

SPECIAL REQUIREMENTS FOR THE POSITION

While job advertisements may state a preference for an undergraduate degree in education, psychology, or sociology, in practice having some demonstrable expertise with information resources in these areas is usually sufficient to be considered for the position, assuming an applicant has all the other required criteria. It's not unheard-of for a subject liaison position for education or psychology at research universities to request an advanced degree in these fields, but prior professional experience supporting those disciplines might well be considered equivalent. Having an educational background in education or psychology might be important when seeking a job with a graduate school that specializes in that one professional field, or a background in psychology might open more doors for applicants for a librarian position in a health care setting, but it's rare for that to be an exclusionary requirement.

MASTER OF LIBRARY SCIENCE AND OTHER COURSEWORK

In addition to core coursework for academic librarianship, MLS students interested in specializing in these fields would be well served by taking courses in: advanced reference, advanced searching, research methods (including research methods for library and information science), thesaurus construction, information-seeking behavior, and library instruction. Should courses be offered in library resources for social and behavioral sciences or health sciences, definitely take advantage of them; an elective in social science statistics—even if taught outside the library and information science program—would also be beneficial. However, students looking to work as a subject specialist in one of these fields in an academic library setting should prioritize the courses aimed at an academic library career first, and the subject specialization second. (Should a need for greater subject knowledge surface after obtaining a job, most college and university settings are open to librarians taking or auditing courses, and that's often more directly relevant to a subject specialist's work than a survey course while a student in an MLS program.)

INTERNSHIPS AND WORK EXPERIENCE

Beyond the core competencies for academic librarianship gained in an MLS program, work experience (whether in paid labor or as a volunteer) and specific projects accomplished will weigh more with potential academic library employers than the content of specific courses taken. Adjunct faculty who are professionals in the desired field may be helpful in getting students into an internship or volunteer situation, should they be lucky to find such a mentor—but it is more common that students have to actively seek out internship opportunities to gain desired practical experience. Besides looking for opportunities to work directly with library patrons (in reference or instructional services), students interested in these fields should consider working with special collections that draw scholars from these disciplines, to gain a working knowledge of issues in these fields and how scholars approach them. Also not to be ignored are formal internships and residencies in related fields (health care, for example) or specific relevant technologies (working with geographic information systems [often referred to as "GIS"], or data management, for example). However, if none of those are in the offing, MLS students shouldn't hesitate to volunteer as unpaid labor (to the extent that's affordable) in a library setting similar to where they want to work, ultimately. Those small(er) professional graduate schools are perennially understaffed and underfunded, and often welcome creative, willing, early-career volunteers.

CAREER PATHS

For the most part, academic librarians specializing in these subject areas have career paths similar to other academic librarians. Because these disciplines are often thought of as the core of social sciences, promotion to a more managerial position as head of reference, or (in a larger research university) supervising all social science librarians is a logical progression. In larger research universities, a sideways career change to positions such as scholarly communications librarian, research methods specialist, or data librarian can also be logical directions from subject specialist in these fields.

Education specialist librarians, particularly those who also have a doctoral degree in education, can sometimes have an advantage in moving into upper-level academic administration positions. They also have job opportunities in K–12 school districts if they also have teacher certification, not just as school librarians but also as managers of district-wide centralized libraries (although these positions usually like to see actual teaching experience as well as teacher certification). It's not uncommon for a sociology, social work, or psychology subject liaison at a college or university to become a library director for one of the professional graduate schools that specialize in these fields. Another possible career path for a subject specialist in psychology is to work for one of the database vendors (e.g., APA, Sage, ProQuest), which need knowledgeable specialists as sales representatives and database developers.

PROFESSIONAL ASSOCIATIONS

Many librarians have found professional associations to be lifelines throughout their careers, the people to turn to when they want to find out best practices, need help with difficult questions, are looking to change jobs or to grow in their positions, and are looking for colleagues. In general they are invaluable sources of professional support. And there are many possible associations for subject specialists in these fields, at levels from national and international organizations to regional and small local groups, so there's no dearth of opportunities to connect with librarian colleagues. Participation is almost always in addition to job responsibilities (with the exceptions that most employers will grant release time to attend meetings, and many fund conference attendance). However, general consensus is that participating in these groups gives a greater return for the extra time and effort spent, both to one's personal professional development and to benefit the workplace (even for the most nonjoining introvert).

There's no obvious way to decide whether it would be more advantageous to actively participate in the larger, national library associations, or to focus more on regional or local professional organizations, or both—it totally depends on individual circumstances. Most will have websites linking resources and will offer e-mail discussion lists, and many have newsletters, blogs, and social media presences—so many of the organizations are listed below are suggested sources of information. Purely for the sake of organization, this list will start with national associations, and move from umbrella organizations to more subject-oriented groups.

National Librarian Organizations

While all academic librarians should be aware of ACRL (the Association of College and Research Libraries division of the American Library Association), some of its sections are particularly useful for subject specialists.

EBSS (Education and Behavioral Sciences Section) has several resources for education specialists, including documents for the Guidelines for Curriculum

Materials Committee (http://www.ala.org/acrl/aboutacrl/directoryofleadership/sections/ebss/ebsswebsite/ebsscommittees/curriculummaterials/cmc). While EBSS' fantastic compendium website Education Librarian's Toolbox (http://wikis.ala.org/acrl/index.php/Education_Librarian's_Toolbox) is aimed at education specialists, its resources will be useful to teaching librarians in all disciplines, too. EBSS also maintains a collection of resources for psychology librarians (http://www.ala.org/acrl/aboutacrl/directoryofleadership/sections/ebss/ebsswebsite/ebsscommittees/curriculummaterials/cmc), and a Social Work Liaison's Toolkit (http://www.ala.org/acrl/aboutacrl/directoryofleadership/sections/ebss/ebsswebsite/socialworksocialwelfare/toolkit). Their Statistical Directory for Education and Social Science Librarians (http://wikis.ala.org/acrl/index.php/A_Statistical_Directory_for_Education_%26_Social_Science_Librarians) is a very useful jumping-off point for locating data relevant to all of these disciplines.

In ACRL's organization, however, sociology is joined with anthropology in ANSS. Their website (https://anssacrl.wordpress.com/) includes links to a downloadable 2010 Assessment Tool for Sociology Collections and Services, as well as useful cataloging and classification resources, database reviews, and bibliographies. Likewise, resources maintained by other sections of ACRL may be very useful to librarians for education, psychology, sociology, and social work. Resources linked from the Women and Gender Studies Section (http://www.libr.org/wgss/) will be helpful for collection development and assessment of electronic database coverage of gender matters and women's issues. Websites for ACRL's Distance Education Section, Instruction Section, Community and Junior Colleges Section, and Colleges Section are all worth perusing regularly.

It's worth a separate notice of ACRL's work on standards, frameworks, and guidelines for academic librarians. These cover several different aspects relevant to subject specialists, but every subject specialist should be familiar with their position papers on information literacy, for example:

- Information Literacy Standards for Teacher Education, http://www.ala.org/acrl/sites/ala.org.acrl/files/content/standards/ilstandards_te.pdf
- Psychology Information Literacy Standards, http://www.ala.org/acrl/standards/psych_info_lit
- Information Literacy Standards for Anthropology and Sociology Students, http://www.ala.org/acrl/standards/anthro_soc_standards
- Information Competencies for Social Work Students, http://www.ala.org/acrl/aboutacrl/directoryofleadership/sections/ebss/ebsswebsite/social/swkpyramid/pyramid

These are frequently updated, and it would be well to be aware of their processes of revision.

The Special Libraries Association includes far more than just corporate and law librarians. Its Social Sciences Division, especially the Public Policy and Nonprofit Sections, may be very useful to librarians working in nongovernmental organizations, nonprofit advocacy agencies, and social services (http://socialscience.sla.org/about-dsoc/). Its Education Division (http://education.sla.org/) offers webinars, lists of relevant reports on education libraries and librarians, and publishes the journal *Education Libraries*.

Librarians supporting teacher education will also want to be aware of what their counterparts in school libraries are doing—and the American Association of School Librarians division of the American Library Association is probably the best resource for that (http://www.ala.org/aasl/).

As for the Medical Library Association, it does have a Mental Health Special Interest Group (home page at http://www6.miami.edu/mhsig/index.html), which provides valuable collection development resources (the Medical Library Association's recommended lists of books and journals for psychology and related fields, and for pharmacology may also be of use, too). The unaffiliated MHLIB discussion list and Association of Mental Health Librarians may also be useful for these fields.

Regional Librarian Groups

Subject specialist librarians in academic settings may find much of value to them from participating in their state's ACRL affiliate organization, their state library association, or their regional Medical Library Association division, although they do not have discipline-related subgroups in the same way as the national counterparts. Depending on one's employer, it may be helpful to become involved in local library consortia, if there is one with similar education or psychology or social work libraries.

International Librarian Groups

The Substance Abuse Librarians and Information Specialists is very active in the United States and Canada, with regular conferences and extensive networking opportunities for librarians working in these fields, particularly around issues of policy, legislation, and treatment.

With a more general focus, IFLA's (International Federation of Library Associations and Institutions) Social Sciences Section offers a blog for its members to talk about their activities at http://blogs.ifla.org/social-science/.

UNESCO's International Committee for Social Science Information and Documentation, as the name implies, works to disseminate social science research information in order to influence policy and inform various worldwide initiatives (http://www.unesco.org/most/icssd.htm).

IASSIST describes itself on its website as "an international organization of professionals working with information technology and data services to support research and teaching in the social sciences." Its quarterly journal is an important source of information on informatics and managing social science research data, and its conferences and member divisions are becoming increasingly influential in these areas (http://www.iassistdata.org/about/index.html).

PUBLICATIONS TO FOLLOW

As mentioned above, the preeminent databases for these fields use their own, fairly elaborate schema for subject terminologies. These have each been published in print, and are also available online. Subject specialists would be well served to have *The Thesaurus of ERIC Descriptors*, *The Thesaurus of Psychological Index Terms* (APA), and the *Thesaurus of Sociological Indexing Terms* close to hand, whether they be as bound volumes or bookmarked websites.

There are too many journals of importance in these subjects to list in this short chapter. Instead, interested readers are referred back to the EBSS resource guides mentioned above in the previous section; to the many LibGuides for education, psychology, psychotherapy, sociology, and social work created by librarian colleagues in these fields; and to these journal lists:

- The American Library Association's Selective List of Journals on Teaching & Learning (http://www.ala.org/acrl/aboutacrl/directoryof leadership/sections/is/iswebsite/projpubs/journalsteachinglearning)
- APA's Library Resources in Psychology web page and links (http://www .apa.org/education/undergrad/library-research.aspx)
- The Medical Library Association's Mental Health Special Interest Group's core list and recommended journals for psychiatry, clinical psychology, and substance abuse (http://www6.miami.edu/mhsig/other .html)

Reviews for books, databases, and online resources for these subject areas are well covered in the standard academic review and collection development sources.

FINAL WORDS

Richard Gaston (2001) writes:

It appears that subject librarians have always performed a liaison role between the library and its client group, the academic departments, and it is this role which distinguishes them from the other functional units within a library organization. The liaison role may explain why subject librarians have survived a multitude of changes in both their working practices (such as IT) and the environment in which they work (such as changes in higher education).

Gaston suggests that the role of subject or liaison librarians has survived the many changes to academic libraries because of the important connection that they provide, built over time (Gaston 2001). This is certainly the case for liaisons in these academic disciplines, and for librarians working in specialized teaching, psychology, or social work settings. Finding library advocates within liaison areas is only part of developing a strong relationship; it is only through mutual support that the relationship will flourish. Students can be more direct about their information needs when they know that their librarian is an expert—and an ally. Many students appreciate time spent in person with their liaison librarian when possible, building relationships organically (particularly around student anxiety with the research process, for those programs that require original research).

Whether working explicitly as a subject liaison for these fields, or working in a branch library for education, psychology, or sociology disciplines or a more generalized social sciences library, or in a specialized professional library setting, librarians with knowledge and expertise in these disciplines have the added satisfaction of actively working toward improving lives in their communities, whether it be through supporting experts in teaching and helping professions, or supporting the training of those professionals. Every reference librarian takes pride in their ability to guide patrons to the information they need—but there's an added glow in knowing that information will be used to help someone who is suffering, or to foster learning. Being a subject specialist in these disciplines can be a heady experience, sometimes.

REFERENCES

Cooke, L. et al. "Evaluating the Impact of Academic Liaison Librarians on their User Community: A Review and Case Study." *New Review of Academic Librarianship* 17, no. 1 (2011): 5–30.

Gaston, R. "The Changing Role of the Subject Librarian, with a Particular Focus on UK Developments, Examined Through a Review of the Literature." *New Review of Academic Librarianship* 7, no. 1 (2001): 19–36.

12 HISTORY, RELIGION, AND PHILOSOPHY LIBRARIANSHIP

Chella Vaidyanathan
Johns Hopkins University

INTRODUCTION

Preparing for a career in librarianship can be an exciting prospect for master of library science (MLS) students and new librarians who are particularly considering becoming subject specialists in the disciplines of history, philosophy, or religion. These three disciplines are integral to the understanding of human society because they address not only the study of past events but also their impact on modern society. Further, they explore the development of various religious beliefs and the investigation of diverse systems of human thoughts and ideas. Therefore scholars in these subjects often grapple with research questions that cross disciplinary boundaries. The three subject areas of history, religion, and philosophy have been grouped together in this chapter for these reasons.

The first step for specializing in one or more of these disciplines is the establishment of a clear career path to help aspiring subject specialists stay on track. This chapter offers practical suggestions for gaining relevant work experience as well as subject expertise, helpful tips for professional development opportunities and staying current in the field, and ideas for upward career mobility.

INTERSECTIONS WITH OTHER DISCIPLINES

A subject specialist librarian often finds that these three subject areas intersect with other fields, such as anthropology, political science, art history, area studies, women and gender studies, literature, music, and the history of science.

For instance, a history librarian may be asked to teach course-integrated library instruction sessions for courses like Cultures of Africa, Cultural History of Enlightenment France, or Feminist Theories. History librarians may find themselves providing in-depth research consultations to scholars working on a wide variety of topics such as the history of the World's Fairs, Marxism, the Black Panther Party, narco-trafficking, or army recruitment posters from the First World War.

Similarly, subject specialists regularly may also find themselves working with other librarians to build and strengthen print, electronic, or special collections in specific research areas such as Victorian Studies, South Asian Studies, May 1968 Protests in France, the Cold War, the History of American Women, or the Cultural and Intellectual History of Europe. The scope of these research areas varies in size; they could be either very broad or quite specific depending on the needs of the researchers. Accordingly, liaison librarians may jointly purchase research materials or team-teach research sessions or workshops with other subject specialists. Thus, the crossing of disciplinary boundaries offers them opportunities to form partnerships and learn from other liaison librarians.

The intersections with other subject areas can lead to the establishment of strong research collections that support the needs of students and faculty in various disciplines. Overall, these cross-disciplinary connections help subject specialists and other library staff members to understand how the various collections support the mission and vision of the libraries while promoting intellectual discourse among the users in the academic as well as nonacademic communities.

Collection development is an important job responsibility for liaison librarians. They play a crucial role in building and developing both the print and digital research collections for their libraries. Often, they may seek input from faculty and graduate students in their assigned subject areas to ensure that the collections meet their research and instruction needs. Specifically, scholars in the history, religious studies, and philosophy disciplines mainly work with print primary sources and historical documents. Hence, they mostly rely on manuscript collections, rare books, diaries, maps, etc., for their research.

WORKPLACES

Many subject specialists or liaison librarians for history, religion, or philosophy may prefer a position in an academic library located in a small liberal arts college or research university. Serving as a liaison librarian involves managing budgets in these subject areas for purchasing books and other research resources, building research collections, working with faculty and students from the departments they support, providing in-depth research consultations for these users, and teaching course-integrated research sessions for undergraduate and graduate students in these disciplines. In addition to subject-specific responsibilities, their duties include offering general reference services at the information or reference desk, or via telephone, e-mail, or chat.

The subject specialist or liaison librarian positions are usually situated within the Department of Academic Liaisons. The nomenclature varies among institutions; they may also be known as the Department of Research and Instruction Services, Department of Information Services, Department of Research Services, or similar titles.

Librarians who prefer to work mainly with historical, religious studies, or philosophical collections may find job openings as curators, special collections librarians, or archivists. Thus, they may work in special collections departments or university archives and museums. These types of positions may involve working with archival collections, printed primary sources, ephemera, or artifacts. These kinds of jobs entail building the special collections in these subject areas, teaching students how to use print primary source materials, and helping researchers locate primary sources related to their research topics.

Likewise, public libraries may offer a variety of positions that suit an aspiring librarian's career interests and academic background. These may involve working with historical or philosophical collections or special collections and archival records within large public libraries. The main difference is that some of the users or researchers may not be from academia. This provides an excellent opportunity for building and developing good relationships with members of the local community.

For librarians with an interest and a subject background in history, positions are available in museums, historical societies, state libraries, or government agencies. Similarly, someone seeking to specialize in religious studies or philosophy may find work in theological or philosophy libraries, which may be located in academic libraries, departments, or seminaries. There may also be independent libraries affiliated with local churches. More information on careers in theological and religious studies libraries can be found at the American Theological Library Association website (https://www.atla.com/).

SPECIAL REQUIREMENTS

Subject specialists and curators generally have a graduate degree in one of the subject areas for which they serve as a liaison librarian. Some humanities librarians have graduate degrees in several areas relevant to their liaison work. For example, archivists are required to have specialized training in archives and records management, and curators and special collections librarians need specialized knowledge related to the history of the book, book illustration processes, the history of bookbinding, medieval manuscripts, and so on.

Proficiency in one or more of the classical or modern languages such as Greek, Latin, French, German, or Italian would also be highly useful for these professionals. These are examples of language skills that may be required for some of the positions. The language requirements may vary depending on the subject areas. A strong background in the subject areas helps to better understand the user groups' disciplinary research and instruction needs. To help undergraduate and graduate students refine their research topics and develop effective research strategies, it is advantageous to have expertise in the subject as well as language skills. These are also crucial for building and strengthening research collections that support the needs of users.

Faculty members in the humanities discipline are increasingly interested in using new digital tools, along with traditional research methods, for teaching students as well as conducting their own research. Scholarly endeavors in this area are collectively defined as the "digital humanities," or simply DH. In his guide to DH, Josh Honn (2012) synthesizes the definition of DH to include "scholarship presented in digital form(s), scholarship enabled by digital methods and tools, scholarship about digital technology and culture, scholarship building and experimenting with digital technology, [and] scholarship critical of its own digitalness." These new digital skills and tools may include, for example, text mining, project management, curating digital exhibits, metadata tagging, programming languages, topic modeling, storyboarding, video editing, Scalar, WordPress, Omeka, geographic information systems, and so on.

In terms of experience, some positions may require one to two years of prior work experience in similar roles. Positions in major research libraries may require three or more years of appropriate experience so that the subject specialist would be able to thoroughly understand and meet the needs of the respective user groups. Other important requirements include good presentation and teaching skills. Previous experience in teaching and presenting at academic conferences would be valuable for subject specialists in performing their duties efficiently.

Job announcements and association websites are great sources of information for learning about special requirements for subject specialist positions. These give an idea about the kinds of job openings available and the necessary special skills required to succeed in those positions. MLS students can benefit from reading job announcements for several months before they begin to apply for positions. This practice helps them learn what skills and experience employers expect, while there's still time to take additional courses or participate in additional internships or work experiences. Good places to check on a regular basis include the following:

- American Library Association Job List: http://joblist.ala.org/
- Libraries Section of Higher Ed Jobs: https://www.higheredjobs.com/admin/search.cfm?JobCat=34
- Job, Residency, and Internship Listings from the Association of Research Libraries: http://www.arl.org/leadership-recruitment/job-listings#.VPIGv-Ee2J8
- INALJ (I Need A Library Job): http://inalj.com/
- The American Association for State and Local History lists internships and positions with historical collections of all types across the United States: http://about.aaslh.org/jobs/
- The American Theological Library Association Job Openings: https://www.atla.com/Members/development/jobs/Pages/default.aspx

- The Rare Books and Manuscripts Section (RBMS) of the Association of College and Research Libraries (ACRL): http://rbms.info/

MASTER OF LIBRARY SCIENCE AND OTHER COURSEWORK

After completing the core courses in the MLS program, one can always selectively take practical courses focusing, for example, on collection development, humanities information, archives records management, oral history, discipline-specific research seminars, digital curation, and the history of the book. It may be helpful to check the online course and webinar offerings of American Library Association units, especially RUSA and ACRL. Courses offered by the Library Juice Academy, continuing education opportunities provided by the Society of American Archivists, and courses offered by the Rare Book School may also prove useful to librarians in history, religion, and philosophy. For oral history courses, check out the workshops taught online by the Institute for Oral History at Baylor University (http://www.baylor.edu/oralhistory/).

For those who have already earned an MLS, it would be beneficial to get a relevant master's degree in history, religious studies, or philosophy depending on one's area of professional interest. Students planning on pursuing an MLS program may want to investigate the dual degrees and specializations offered by library schools at different universities. Someone currently pursuing a library science degree might check to see if his or her institution offers dual-degree programs. At the time of this writing, the following institutions provide dual degrees and other specializations:

- History and Library Science Dual-Degree Program, College of Information Studies, University of Maryland, College Park
- School of Informatics and Computing, Indiana University Bloomington
- New York University's Graduate School of Arts and Science and Long Island University's Palmer School of Library and Information Science
- Joint Degree Programs, The Catholic University of America
- Dual Degrees, School of Information and Library Science, University of North Carolina at Chapel Hill

Professional librarians (who have completed their MLS) may want to enroll in a graduate program at the academic institution where they are currently employed. Some employers offer generous tuition assistance and flexible work schedules to help their employees complete degree programs. Additionally, it is essential to complete language courses germane to the subject specialist's areas of interest as applicable to history, religious studies, or philosophy.

For anyone interested in becoming a curator, special collections librarian, or archivist, the following resources would be very helpful in learning about the profession in general, necessary educational background, and pertinent courses and skills:

- Career FAQs, Rare Books and Manuscripts Section: http://rbms.info/careers-faq/ (Allison Clemens, ed., Careers FAQ, Rare Books and Manuscripts Section, ACRL, 2014)
- Rare Book School, especially their courses offered in several locations: http://www.rarebookschool.org/
- Society of American Archivists: "So You Want to Be an Archivist: An Overview of the Archives Profession": http://www2.archivists.org/profession

To meet the rising importance of DH and better prepare subject specialists for changing roles, some universities now offer courses on relevant new skills and digital tools. Two well-known settings for learning about DH are the Digital Humanities Summer Institute at the University of Victoria and the Humanities and Technology Camp. Other good resources include *Getting Started in the Digital Humanities* by Lisa Spiro and *How Did They Make That?* by Miriam Posner. These are great resources for subject specialists interested in getting an introduction to DH in general and to DH projects in particular. There are also several active local groups, such as NYC Digital Humanities (http://nycdh.org/) and PhillyDH (http://phillydh.org/), that bring together scholars, practitioners, librarians, archivists, programmers, and technologists to collaborate on and share ideas about DH projects. They also offer workshops that help participants acquire new skills.

INTERNSHIPS AND WORK EXPERIENCE

Practical experience goes hand in hand with theoretical learning and coursework. Internships available in academic, public, and specialized libraries would be invaluable for MLS students. Graduate assistantships offer useful practical training for students interested in humanities librarianships. Museums, local archives, historical societies, and libraries present volunteer opportunities that help in honing skills for the job market. Listing relevant internships, graduate assistantships, and volunteer work on résumés is very helpful in bolstering applications in a competitive job market. Listing new skills acquired during the course of the internships or brief descriptions of responsibilities for the volunteer work would be particularly helpful. Hence, it is a good idea to check the listings on professional associations' websites for internships and volunteering opportunities. Both paid and unpaid internships and volunteer work will usually appear on the website of the institution or organization. However, in some cases unpaid opportunities may not be listed. In such instances, it is always a good idea to approach the archivist, librarian, or curator of that library or department to explore whether unpaid volunteer work can be arranged for internship course credit. The following would be good sites to find information about internship opportunities:

- Job, Residency, and Internship Listings from the Association of Research Libraries: http://www.arl.org/leadership-recruitment/job-listings#.VPIGv-Ee2J8

- Internships and Fellowships: Smithsonian Libraries: http://library.si.edu/internships-and-fellowships
- Jobs, Internships, Fellowships, and Volunteer Opportunities: Library of Congress: http://www.loc.gov/hr/employment/index.php?action=cMain.showFellowships
- Library Science: Pre-Professional (Internships): Drexel University College of Computing and Informatics: http://drexel.edu/cci/resources/career-services/job-search-tool/library-science/pre-professional/
- Presidential Libraries Internship Opportunities: National Archives: http://www.archives.gov/careers/internships/libraries.html
- The American Association for State and Local History lists internships and positions with historical collections of all types across the United States: http://about.aaslh.org/jobs/
- Internship Roster: Art Libraries Society of North America (ARLIS/NA): https://www.arlisna.org/career-resources/internship-roster
- Job and Internship Opportunities: Columbia University Libraries: http://library.columbia.edu/about/jobs-internships.html
- Internships and Practica in the University of Colorado Boulder Libraries: University of Colorado Boulder Libraries: http://ucblibraries.colorado.edu/librarianship/Internships/internship.htm

Moreover, finding good mentors and requesting guidance from them to embark on the chosen career track is highly advantageous. New librarians seeking to develop subject expertise may offer to help at the main reference/information desk or at the reference desk located in special collections. They can set annual goals that focus on building and developing new collections, which may involve working with colleagues in the Department of Special Collections. They can also seek experienced mentors within and outside of their institutions or organizations to learn about the new career paths they are interested in. Often, mentors are very happy to share information about their careers and help new librarians reach their professional goals. Webinars and online courses also provide opportunities to learn new skills and develop proficiency.

CAREER PATHS

Traditional career paths for humanities librarians may include eventually ascending to a leadership position in the Department of Academic Liaisons (or similar), where one would be in charge of supervising, managing, and leading the other academic liaisons. Likewise, another career goal might be to achieve a leadership position in special collections or become the university archivist. With the developments in the field of DH, some professionals may be more interested in becoming technologically proficient, which may lead to positions such as the director of an institution's DH center or director of research and scholarship or digital collections. It may be possible to find similar positions for upward mobility in public, state, or special libraries.

PROFESSIONAL ORGANIZATIONS

Participation in professional organizations and committee work is indispensable for staying current in the field and learning to adapt to changes. It is also a way of giving back to the profession by sharing knowledge and subject expertise with colleagues from other institutions and organizations. Professional contribution helps in building good social and professional networks that may be helpful for future career advancement.

With regard to specific professional groups, the RUSA History Section is ideal for history librarians. Religious studies and philosophy librarians can join the American Theological Library Association and the Philosophical, Religious, and Theological Studies Discussion Group of the ACRL. Depending on their subject specialties, job responsibilities, personal interests, and career aspirations, humanities librarians may choose to join one or more of the following: the Western European Studies Section (WESS) of the ACRL; Asian African and Middle Eastern Section (AAMES) of the ACRL; Rare Books and Manuscripts Section (RBMS) of the ACRL; Instruction Section (IS) of the ACRL; American Historical Association; American Philosophical Association; American Academy of Religion; Digital Humanities Interest Group of ACRL; Digital Curation Interest Group of the ACRL; Digital Scholarship Centers Interest Group of the ACRL; Society of American Archivists; Humanities, Arts, Science, and Technology Alliance and Collaboratory; and Alliance of Digital Humanities Organizations.

PUBLICATIONS TO FOLLOW

To stay current in the field, it is necessary to choose and regularly read four to five publications from discipline-related associations, library associations, and interest groups. Some of these are *The American Historical Review, Perspectives on History, Journal of the American Academy of Religion, Religious Studies News, Proceedings of the American Philosophical Society, American Libraries, Booklist, Library Technology Reports, Reference & User Services Quarterly, College and Research Libraries News, College & Research Libraries, CHOICE: Current Reviews for Academic Libraries, RBM: A Journal of Rare Books, Manuscripts, and Cultural Heritage, Journal of Digital Humanities, Digital Humanities Quarterly, DHCommons Journal, American Archivist,* and *Archival Outlook.*

FINAL WORDS

There are numerous possibilities for those who wish to be subject specialists in history, religion, or philosophy. An academic environment would provide enjoyable interactions with faculty, students, and scholars from various fields. Public or special libraries would provide the chance to work with a wide variety of patrons including research scholars, local community members, schoolchildren, and the general public. Furthermore, there are several options for professional development and networking with colleagues who share the same passion for these subject areas. And finally, it is vital to subscribe to professional listservs and be active via Twitter, Facebook, and other social media sites to stay updated on the latest developments in the field.

REFERENCES AND SELECTED READINGS

Arthur, Paul Longley, and Katherine Bode. *Advancing Digital Humanities: Research, Methods, Theories*. Houndmills, Basingstoke, Hampshire: Palgrave Macmillan, 2014.

Association of Research Libraries, CNI, and Scholarly Publishing and Academic Resources Coalition. *Research Library Issues* 265 (August 2009): *Special Issue on Liaison Librarian Roles*. ARL Digital Publications, 2009.

Cohen, Daniel J., and Roy Rosenzweig. *Digital History: A Guide to Gathering, Preserving, and Presenting the Past on the Web*. Philadelphia: University of Pennsylvania Press, 2006.

Cohen, Daniel J., and Tom Scheinfeldt. *Hacking the Academy: New Approaches to Scholarship and Teaching from Digital Humanities*. Ann Arbor: University of Michigan Press, 2013.

Crawford, Alice. *New Directions for Academic Liaison Librarians*. Oxford: Chandos, 2012.

Deegan, Marilyn, and Willard McCarty. *Collaborative Research in the Digital Humanities*. Farnham, Surrey, England: Ashgate, 2011.

Dougherty, Jack, and Kristen Nawrotzki. *Writing History in the Digital Age*. Ann Arbor: University of Michigan Press, 2013.

Galgano, Michael J., J. Chris Arndt, and Raymond M. Hyser. *Doing History: Research and Writing in the Digital Age*. 2nd ed. Boston: Wadsworth Cengage Learning, 2013.

Gold, Matthew K. *Debates in the Digital Humanities*. Minneapolis: University of Minnesota Press, 2012.

Hirsch, Brett D. *Digital Humanities Pedagogy: Practices, Principles and Politics*. Cambridge: OpenBook, 2012.

Honn, Josh. *A Guide to Digital Humanities*. 2012. Accessed February 5, 2015. http://sites.northwestern.edu/guidetodh/.

Jaguszewski, Janice M., and Williams, Karen. *New Roles for New Times: Transforming Liaison Roles in Research Libraries*. Chicago: ARL Digital Publications, 2013.

Jones, Steven E. *The Emergence of the Digital Humanities*. New York: Routledge, 2014.

Kelly, T. Mills. *Teaching History in the Digital Age*. Ann Arbor: University of Michigan Press, 2013.

Kitchens, Joel D. *Librarians, Historians, and New Opportunities for Discourse: A Guide for Clio's Helpers*. Santa Barbara, CA: Libraries Unlimited, 2012.

Lünen, Alexander von, and Charles Travis. *History and GIS: Epistemologies, Considerations and Reflections*. Dordrecht, Netherlands: Springer, 2013.

Mack, Daniel C., and Gary W. White. *Assessing Liaison Librarians: Documenting Impact for Positive Change*. Chicago: Association of College and Research Libraries, 2014.

Mitchell, Eleanor, Peggy Seiden, and Suzy Taraba. *Past or Portal? Enhancing Undergraduate Learning Through Special Collections and Archives*. Chicago: Association of College and Research Libraries, 2012.

Moniz, Richard, Jo Henry, and Joe Eshleman. *Fundamentals for the Academic Liaison*. Chicago: American Library Association, 2014.

Perrault, Anna H., Elizabeth Smith Aversa, and Ron Blazek. *Information Resources in the Humanities and the Arts*. 6th ed. Santa Barbara, CA: Libraries Unlimited, 2013.

Posner, Miriam. *How Did They Make That?* (blog). http://miriamposner.com/blog/how-did-they-make-that/.

Presnell, Jenny L. *The Information-Literate Historian: A Guide to Research for History Students*. New York: Oxford University Press, 2007.

Rosenzweig, Roy. *Clio Wired: The Future of the Past in the Digital Age*. New York: Columbia University Press, 2011.

Spiro, Lisa. *Getting Started in the Digital Humanities* (blog). https://digitalscholarship.wordpress.com/.

Terras, Melissa M., Julianne Nyhan, and Edward Vanhoutte, eds. *Defining Digital Humanities: A Reader*. Farnham, Surrey, England: Ashgate; Burlington, VT: Ashgate, 2013.

Theimer, Kate, ed. *Description: Innovative Practices for Archives and Special Collections*. Lanham, MD: Rowman & Littlefield, 2014.

Theimer, Kate, ed. *Outreach: Innovative Practices for Archives and Special Collections*. Lanham, MD: Rowman & Littlefield, 2014.

Theimer, Kate, ed. *Reference and Access: Innovative Practices for Archives and Special Collections*. Lanham, MD: Rowman & Littlefield, 2014.

Walter, Scott, and Karen Williams. *The Expert Library: Staffing, Sustaining, and Advancing the Academic Library in the 21st Century*. Chicago: Association of College and Research Libraries, 2010.

Whittaker, Beth M., and Lynne M. Thomas. *Special Collections 2.0: New Technologies for Rare Books, Manuscripts, and Archival Collections*. Santa Barbara, CA: Libraries Unlimited.

13   BUSINESS LIBRARIANSHIP

Diane Zabel
Penn State University

INTRODUCTION

This chapter is an introduction to the fast-paced specialty of business librarianship. This career path requires librarians to learn business vocabulary and advanced business concepts, and to have the ability to handle demanding clientele who expect quick and expert responses to complex queries.

To give readers a flavor of the range of questions a business librarian might be asked to answer (especially one working in an academic setting), here is a sampling of questions that this author has been asked by students:

- What is Walmart's sustainability strategy?
- Is Starbuck's coffee ethically sourced?
- How will global warming and climate change impact the ski industry—here and abroad?
- What are the projected same-store sales for Chipotle?
- I need data on the global candy industry, especially the market for China and India. What companies already have a presence in these markets? By the way, what kinds of chocolate products are likely to sell well in these countries?
- Can you help me expand on the impact of Airbnb and other home-sharing services? Specifically, what is the impact on the lodging industry?

- I am an entrepreneurship student working on a business plan for a nutritional supplement company. I need market research (size, financials, pricing, key players, etc.).
- Can you help me put together a profile of the typical Nascar fan? Also, what's the most effective way to market to these consumers?
- Is there a relationship between credit-based insurance scores and insurance losses? Is it ethical to use this relationship in rating and underwriting?
- We are a team of engineering and business students working on a project. Our goal is to design a prototype of a low-cost water drill to be used in East Africa. We need help analyzing this industry. We also need information about doing business in Africa.

These questions reflect some trends. Trends are changes in behavior, attitudes, or expected patterns (which might range from changes in home ownership rates to changes in family size). Students are interested in researching topics relating to sustainability and green business. They are interested in green initiatives, green practices and technologies, green products, and green careers. There is also tremendous interest in entrepreneurship and starting your own business. This is not surprising given the growth of entrepreneurship courses across the curriculum. However, what is significant is the interdisciplinary approach to entrepreneurship. Students are working in teams that deliberately bring together students from different fields. Another trend is an increased interest in ethical behavior. Students are concerned with issues ranging from the impact of corporate fraud to ethical issues surrounding the sourcing of raw materials. Students also understand that this is a global economy. They need resources that cover emerging markets or provide a global perspective. Students also understand the importance of a service economy. Many students (not only those enrolled in hospitality or tourism management programs) ask questions about the restaurant, lodging, tourism, and recreation industries given the importance of these sectors in the U.S. economy. These sample questions convey that students are asking complex questions requiring sophisticated resources that bring together company information, industry analyses, market data, and competitive intelligence.

There is also a huge push to teach students the importance of company and industry research in a career context. This author conducts many instructional sessions around the topics of career exploration and job hunt. Even master of business administration students need to learn about occupational concentrations. What do supply chain managers do? What does a brand manager do? What are these occupations like in terms of salary, setting, variety, intensity, and lifestyle? What training, exams, or certifications are required or valued? It is important to give students the skills to target the best possible employers. They have to be able to present themselves as knowledgeable potential hires that are well informed about the company and the industry. This emphasis on resources and services to assist job seekers is also a priority for librarians working in public libraries.

CORE AREAS OF KNOWLEDGE

There are three main components of business research: company research; industry and market research; and environmental scanning. Librarians must have a basic understanding of how companies are organized. Companies are classified as being publicly traded or privately held. Publicly traded companies (such as Hershey, ExxonMobil, PepsiCo, Apple, Johnson & Johnson, and Delta Air Lines) are required by law to disclose information to shareholders and the government. In contrast, private companies (which range from small locally owned businesses to well-known national firms such as Mars, Dell, and Toys "R" Us) have no obligation to disclose financial or operational information. Consequently, it is much easier to research publicly traded companies than privately held companies. However, the concept of proprietary information is a key one in business librarianship. Proprietary information is data not shared by a company. For example, even publicly traded companies do not have to report detailed information about operations, such as manufacturing processes.

When helping a patron research a company, it is not unusual for a librarian to search for the following pieces of information: a company's status and structure (i.e., public or private; parent or subsidiary); ticker symbol if publicly traded; line of business; specific products and services (sometimes expressed as brands); location of headquarters; names (and sometimes biographical profiles) of principal officers; date founded; brief corporate history; number of employees; geographic reach; mission; values; corporate culture; strategic direction; marketing strategy; market share; financial performance; rank within the industry; major competitors; new developments (i.e., products in the pipeline; mergers; acquisitions; expansion into new geographic markets); problems and challenges (i.e., declining sales; rising commodity prices; disruptions in the supply chain; lawsuits or pending litigation); and outlook for the next three to five years.

Librarians will be able to master these typical questions with experience, especially if they have taken a business reference course as part of their master of library science (MLS) program. Additionally, they may want to enroll in "Business Reference 101," an online course offered by the Reference and User Services Association, a division of the American Library Association. Business librarians will also find Celia Ross's practical manual, *Making Sense of Business Reference: A Guide for Librarians and Research Professionals*, to be an invaluable resource.

The second main component of business research, industry research, is a natural extension of company research. It is vital to supplement company information with information about the industry in which a firm competes. The following industry-wide data is often sought after by patrons: an indication of the size of an industry; key companies; the industry code (referred to as the North American Industrial Classification System, or NAICS, code); the economic health of the overall industry as well as segments of the industry; industry news; outlook for the industry; and trends impacting the industry (which might range from increased consolidation to increased government regulation). Market data supplement industry data. Researchers want to create a profile of who uses or might use a product or service, information often accessible in commercial databases that contain market research reports. Researchers also need to identify lucrative markets. This is more complex than locating consumption and demographic data. Companies that are expanding (especially internationally) need to learn about the business climate, infrastructure, workforce, and hurdles to doing business in a specific geographic location.

Environmental scanning, the third major component of business research, requires the most creativity on the part of librarians who are assisting patrons. This is a technique commonly used in business, and one taught throughout the business curriculum in strategic planning and management courses. In the real world, managers examine economic, demographic, social, political, technological, and legislative changes or proposed changes that might signal opportunities or threats. Here are some examples of developments or potential developments that a manager might monitor:

- A growing middle class in China, India, and other countries
- The growing importance of the Millennial generation in the marketplace and the workplace
- A growing interest in healthy lifestyle choices, from diet to exercise
- The impact of proposed changes to the Affordable Care Act
- The impact of data breaches on mobile commerce
- Increased nutritional product labeling

Some of these developments are examples of trends. Librarians and other researchers can detect trends by browsing a variety of newspapers, popular magazines, and business magazines. Another technique for tracking trends is to monitor what is trending on the Internet, Facebook, Twitter, and other social media.

Librarians wanting to develop a better sense of environmental scanning might want to study how their own professional organizations have used environmental scanning as a technique to plan for the future. For example, OCLC (whose membership includes libraries, museums, and archives) often looks at social, economic, technological, and research and learning changes that have major implications for academic and public libraries. More information about OCLC's findings can be found on the organization's website (http://www.oclc.org). The American Library Association (http://www.ala.org) has also used environmental scanning as part of its strategic planning process. The American Library Association's Association of College and Research Libraries reports on the U.S. academic library environment every two years in its *ACRL Environmental Scan*, published every two years.

INTERSECTIONS WITH OTHER DISCIPLINES

Business may be the most interdisciplinary social science due to the multilayered nature of many business queries. An understanding of economic indicators and basic economic concepts is essential. It is not unusual to search for domestic and global data relating to income, employment, wages, inflation, consumer prices, gross domestic product, and economic growth rates. Additionally, academic business librarians may find that their job duties have been expanded to include responsibility for economics. Since economic data is often collected by governmental agencies, business librarians often consult with colleagues whose specialty is government information. Librarians also need a basic understanding of legal resources in order to handle queries dealing with business activities that are subject to the law. Business also has linkages to psychology. While managers want to know what motivates employees, marketers want to know what motivates people to buy a product or service. Business researchers are also interested in learning what sociologists know about changing demographic shifts, changing attitudes, and other broad societal changes. This knowledge can help researchers identify the demand for new products and services. Since researchers are interested in place, there are linkages to geography. Businesses invest a lot of time and effort when making decisions about site locations. Geographic data can help businesses compare geographic markets before making site decisions. Since researchers sometimes need historical data (such as information on past economic booms and busts or the impact of an event on stock prices), an understanding of basic historical resources is helpful. Business even has linkages to the humanities. Since ethics is integrated across the business curriculum (from accounting to supply chain management), it is helpful to be aware of sources in philosophy that cover ethics.

Business has close linkages to applied sciences such as computer science, statistics, and mathematics. Students enrolled in management information systems programs need an understanding of database design. Although all fields of business are data driven, actuarial science students make extensive use of statistics. Actuarial science, finance, and supply chain majors often use advanced mathematics for modeling. Business also has linkages to engineering. Supply chain students often have questions about manufacturing processes, which relates to industrial engineering. They also need transportation data, another subfield of engineering. Finally, it is not uncommon for a business librarian to use architectural resources that provide construction costs. A range of business students, from supply chain students to real estate students, may need to know the cost of constructing buildings ranging from warehouses to retail stores.

WORKPLACES

There are many employers of business specialists: academic, public, corporate, and other special libraries (such as those affiliated with governmental agencies). An academic business librarian might work as a business specialist in a team of public services librarians or be one of several specialists in a separate subject library focusing on business. The organizational structure of business libraries varies. Some business libraries are units within a larger academic library. Other academic business libraries are independent from central library administration. In these cases, the library is often physically located in the business school and librarians report to business school administration. There is also a hybrid model with librarians reporting to both the business school and central library administration. However, regardless of physical location or reporting structure, academic business librarians across the country are busy experimenting with service models. For example, this author's library offers onsite consultation in the atrium of the business college. Librarians have been rebranded as research consultants and assist students with course assignments, background research for case competitions, and interview preparation for internships and jobs.

In many public libraries, the business librarian is often a general reference librarian who has been designated as the specialist for business. Larger public libraries may have a business center or division. Regardless of structure or size, community outreach is key. The business librarian will be expected to develop and maintain relationships with the local business community. A growing number of public libraries have become centers for entrepreneurial activity. Readers wanting to gain insight into business librarianship in public libraries should consult Andersen's excellent article (2008) on this topic (see the References section).

Corporate librarianship has also been an option for business librarians. A corporate librarian may be a solo librarian working in an advertising agency or one of several librarians working in a research department of a large financial services firm. Librarians with business expertise may also be employed in law firms. Those interested in learning more about corporate librarianship are advised to consult Rimland and Masuchika's insightful article (2008) on this career path (see the References section).

SPECIAL REQUIREMENTS

What skills are employers looking for in business librarians? This author collected about a dozen job postings while working on this chapter. The majority of these ads were recruitments for academic librarians. A quick analysis of these announcements suggest that academic employers regard the following skills as basic qualifications:

- Experience using commercial databases relevant to business and economics
- Experience providing business reference, both in-person and online
- Strong problem-solving skills
- Strong analytical skills
- Excellent interpersonal skills
- Excellent verbal and written communication skills
- Fluency with emerging technologies relevant to librarianship

Several traits were commonly listed as requirements, including the following:

- Being able to work independently
- Being able to work collaboratively

- Being open to new ideas
- Having a strong service orientation
- Being creative
- Being innovative
- Being flexible
- Being committed to developing professionally

These employers also listed preferred qualifications, including the following:

- An academic background (undergraduate degree, graduate degree, or coursework) in business, economics, or social sciences
- Experience delivering library instruction or library workshops
- Experience creating research guides, tutorials, or other learning objects
- Experience with collection development
- Being proficient at finding and using statistics and data sets
- Familiarity with standard software packages used for statistical analysis

It appears that employers are rather flexible regarding years of experience. Several of these ads listed two years of professional experience (either in a business or academic library) as a minimum requirement. One announcement listed zero to one year of experience. Some positions did not require any previous professional experience, appearing to target recent graduates. Only one position stated a preference for candidates with three to five years of professional experience in an academic or corporate library.

In this short time frame, this author was able to collect only a very small number of job postings for business librarians in public libraries and corporate settings. Positions in public libraries seemed to be less prescriptive regarding qualifications. Emphasis seemed to be placed on outreach skills. Job postings for corporate librarians seemed to emphasize the need for knowledge of relevant databases.

MASTER OF LIBRARY SCIENCE AND OTHER COURSEWORK

While almost all of the academic job postings that this author looked at required a master's degree in library science from an American Library Association–accredited school (or an equivalent degree), this was not listed as a requirement for all of the public and corporate library positions she was able to examine. However, when reviewing responsibilities listed in job postings, it would be advantageous for students to complete the following coursework:

- A course focused on business reference
- A course on reference in the social sciences, including the basics of legal research
- A course on government information
- A course on information literacy and instruction

- A course on collection development
- A course on finding and using statistics and data
- A course on statistical analysis that includes working with common software packages used for quantitative analysis

What do you do if these courses are not part of the curriculum of the library school program you are enrolled in? One option is to invest in your professional development by enrolling in online courses or webinars offered by professional associations. For example, the Reference and User Services Association (RUSA), a division of the American Library Association, offers "Business Reference 101," a very popular four-week course that helps beginners become expert business librarians. In 2015 RUSA launched a new online course, "Introduction to Economic Data on the Web." Librarians who are recognized nationally for their expertise teach these courses. More information about these courses and other educational offerings can be found on RUSA's website (http://www.ala.org/rusa).

INTERNSHIPS AND WORK EXPERIENCE

Practical on-the-job experience is highly valued by employers filling positions for business librarians. In some ways, librarianship is unique because it is not uncommon for staff members to move into librarian positions after earning an MLS. Readers who are exploring this career change should read McCallips's reflective article (2008) on transitioning from a staff to faculty librarian position in an academic library (see the References section).

Readers who decided to pursue the MLS degree upon completion of their undergraduate degree are strongly advised to obtain work experience in the form of a graduate assistantship, internship, or practicum. The ideal candidate for a business librarian position would have experience working in an academic business library or in a large public library that handles a significant volume of business reference transactions. Other valued experience would include working in a large public services unit of an academic library that handles an array of questions, including business queries.

Some individuals take time out to work in nonlibrary settings before pursuing the MLS degree. Experience in the corporate setting is highly valued. Individuals who have worked in corporate positions requiring research and writing bring valuable skills to business librarianship. Many business librarians are career changers. A significant percentage of business librarians have prior business-related work experience. Hines and Baker's article (2008) on business librarians' prior work experience and career choices provides fascinating data on the employment history of business librarians (see the References section).

CAREER PATHS

The career path for academic business librarians is most likely to be influenced by the status of librarians within a specific college or university.

Those librarians with faculty status will need to focus on meeting the tenure and promotion requirements for their institution. Upon earning tenure, some business librarians find that they have the time to pursue a master of business administration or other advanced degree. Other business librarians may take advantage of opportunities to teach as adjuncts in nearby or online master of library and information science programs. Librarians who are seriously thinking about taking on this challenge should read LeBeau's excellent chapter (2011) on the demands and rewards of adjunct teaching (see the References section). Business librarianship also prepares librarians to move into senior-level leadership positions. It is not uncommon for heads of major business libraries to be recruited for associate university librarian positions.

Business librarians in public and corporate library settings may advance to department head, division head, or director positions after gaining experience. However, some will choose to transition to academic libraries. Those librarians thinking of making this career move should read LeBeau's article (2008) on transitioning to academic libraries (see the References section). This article also discusses the need for more seasoned business librarians to serve as adjuncts in MLS programs.

PROFESSIONAL ORGANIZATIONS

Professional organizations play an important role in helping business librarians keep abreast of new products, develop leadership skills, and network with other business librarians. RUSA has an entire section, the Business Reference and Services Section (BRASS), that brings together academic, public, and corporate business librarians. BRASS is a vibrant organization that has a wealth of tools for new and experienced business librarians, including the following: professional standards in the form of "Guidelines for Business Information Responses"; BRASS-L, a discussion list that provides news about BRASS activities as well as job postings; *Academic BRASS*, an online newsletter about topics relating to academic business librarianship; *Public Libraries Briefcase*, an online newsletter focusing on topics relating to business reference services in public libraries; and "BRASS Business Guides," a series of over 20 research guides covering topics ranging from accounting to sports management. Access to these tools and other BRASS resources is provided via BRASS's website (http://www .ala.org/rusa/sections/brass). BRASS also provides many leadership and networking opportunities, as there are almost 20 committees to serve on.

Another important professional organization for business librarians is the Special Libraries Association (SLA). SLA has a Business and Finance Division, which includes the following sections: Advertising and Marketing; College and University Business Librarians; Corporate Information Centers; and Financial Services. There is also a round table for librarians who focus on the hospitality industry. SLA's Business & Finance Division provides continuing education and networking opportunities. It also has an active mentoring program. More information about this division can be found on SLA's website (http://bf.sla.org).

Business librarians who want to learn more about data may want to consider joining the International Association for Social Science Information Services and Technology (IASSIST). This group's small size (about 300 members) makes it easy for librarians to network with other professionals who support data services. IASSIST sponsors an annual conference. The organization also publishes *IASSIST Quarterly*, an open-access peer-reviewed journal. More information about this organization can be found on its website (http://www.iassistdata.org).

PUBLICATIONS TO FOLLOW

Many of the publications to follow in business librarianship are published by leading professional organizations. *Reference & User Services Quarterly* (often referred to as "*RUSQ*") is the referreed journal published by RUSA. In addition to publishing scholarly articles, practical columns, and book reviews, it includes articles about the work of RUSA's sections, including BRASS. *RUSQ* publishes "Best of the Best Business Websites" and "Outstanding Business Reference Resources"; both are products from BRASS.

SLA's Business & Finance Division publishes *The Bulletin*. This contains news about the division, practical articles about business librarianship, and book reviews.

In February 2015, the Academic Business Library Directors group announced the debut of *Ticker: The Academic Business Librarianship Review*. Academic Business Library Directors is an organization for directors of academic business libraries that support preeminent business schools in the United States and Canada. According to the journal's website (http://ticker.mcgill.ca/), *Ticker*'s mission is to provide "a forum for the exchange of the research, best practices, and innovative thinking in business librarianship and business library management." The scope will include "articles, thought pieces, member profiles, case studies, and conference reports."

There is also an important commercially published journal in the field of business librarianship: the *Journal of Business & Finance Librarianship*. This quarterly journal publishes practitioner-oriented articles, scholarly research based articles, and in-depth book and database reviews.

FINAL WORDS

This author can't imagine a more rewarding specialty than business librarianship. Even after three decades of academic librarianship, she can still be stumped by a business reference question. The good news is that she can call upon talented and generous business librarians across the country for guidance. There is a genuine feeling of community among business librarians. Looking forward, she thinks that agility is the trait that is particularly needed by business librarians, especially those working in academic settings. Since business school curriculum changes to meet the needs of business, academic business librarians need to be agile. They need to be able to build collections and develop resources on the fly to support emerging areas of business and economics. Academic business librarians will also be asked to spend more of their time creating resources that support online learners, a growing user population. There will also be growing pressure for business librarians to be good financial stewards by rigorously evaluating the merits of their library's resources on an ongoing basis, especially given the high cost of many business databases. These responsibilities and more make business librarianship an intellectually challenging specialty.

REFERENCES

American Library Association. Accessed July 22, 2015. http://www.ala.org.

Andersen, Mark E. "Taking Business (Librarianship) Public." *Journal of Business & Finance Librarianship* 13, no. 3 (2008): 311–19.

Business Reference and Services Section. Accessed July 22, 2015. http://www.ala.org/rusa/sections/brass.

Hines, Todd M., and Amia L. Baker. "The Career Choices of Business Librarians: A Survey and Discussion." *Journal of Business & Finance Librarianship* 13, no. 3 (2008): 391–404.

International Association for Social Science Information and Technology. Accessed July 22, 2015. http://www.iassistdata.org.

LeBeau, Christopher. "Practitioners as Adjunct Teachers." In *Reference Reborn: Breathing New Life into Public Services Librarianship*, edited by Diane Zabel, 355–71. Santa Barbara, CA: Libraries Unlimited, 2011.

LeBeau, Christopher. "Transitions to Academic Libraries for Business Librarians and Librarians' Response to Adjunct Teaching." *Journal of Business & Finance Librarianship* 13, no. 3 (2008): 295–309.

McCallips, Cheryl. "Transition from Staff to Faculty in an Academic Library." *Journal of Business & Finance Librarianship* 13, no. 3 (2008): 287–93.

OCLC. Accessed July 22, 2015. http://www.oclc.org.

Reference and User Services Association. Accessed July 22, 2015. http://www.ala.org/rusa.

Rimland, Emily, and Glenn Masuchika. "Transitioning to Corporate Librarianship." *Journal of Business & Finance Librarianship* 13, no. 3 (2008): 321–34.

14 HEALTH SCIENCES LIBRARIANSHIP

Dixie A. Jones
Louisiana State University Shreveport

INTRODUCTION

Health sciences librarianship includes not only medicine but also dentistry, nursing, pharmacy, veterinary medicine, chiropractic medicine, physical therapy, occupational therapy, and other allied health fields. Thus, current nomenclature is often "health sciences librarianship" rather than "medical librarianship" to be inclusive of the many health-related areas in addition to medicine. Having established that, the terms "medical" and "health sciences" will be used interchangeably in this chapter. Health sciences librarianship can encompass the biological sciences as well as psychology, both of which are covered in other chapters in this text. Library and information practitioners in the health sciences use the same principles for organizing literature and searching literature as do practitioners in other disciplines and, as with other disciplines, must have working knowledge of the subject matter, familiarity with the terminology, and expertise in using or searching the specialized literature in the health sciences areas that they serve.

Health sciences librarianship is an intellectually stimulating specialty for information professionals. If one is curious about how the body works at the molecular level or how cancer treatments are explored, this sphere of librarianship might be a good fit! Medicine and other health-related sciences are rapidly evolving and are highly dependent on the most current, accurate information. Medical librarians, depending on their employment settings, may have opportunities to work with a variety of clientele—consumers, the aged, children, health care providers, other members of the medical team, researchers, faculty members, students, and others. Librarians specializing in the health sciences might help clinicians find evidence in the literature to effectively treat patients with rare problems, i.e., not typical, textbook conditions. They might conduct literature searches using specialized databases, or make decisions about which health sciences resources to purchase, or work with medical history collections or archives. Those who work with archival materials, such as historical papers or old surgical instruments can combine a love of history and health sciences librarianship. The resources used by health information professionals are rapidly evolving. The journal literature is changing with the addition of new formats, such as online videos of surgical procedures rather than traditional articles on surgical techniques or the posting of supplementary materials on websites rather than in the journal issues where the associated articles appear.

Health sciences librarianship has its own code of ethics. The Medical Library Association (MLA) "Code of Ethics for Health Sciences Librarianship" (2010) serves as a guide for health information professionals. The specialty also has its own national library. Health information professionals benefit from the products and services of the National Library of Medicine (NLM), a division of the National Institutes of Health. NLM coordinates an interlibrary loan system for medical libraries (DOCLINE), provides a classification system for medical materials, creates and maintains a number of free databases, and supports a regional network system that delivers resources and education to both health sciences librarians and the public.

INTERSECTIONS WITH OTHER DISCIPLINES

As mentioned in the first paragraph, there are a number of specialties that fall under the wide umbrella of health sciences librarianship, e.g., veterinary librarianship and dentistry. Biological sciences, a subject area closely related to medicine, can be an area of specialization for librarians in academic and research settings and is addressed in another chapter in this text. Librarians who specialize in mental health resources might work with the literature of psychiatry in medical settings or with the literature of psychology, which is also addressed elsewhere in this book. Health informatics is an area that specifically involves application of computer technology to the health care information field. People in a number of different professions practice health informatics; librarianship is one of these professions and a number of library schools offer courses in health or medical informatics. Another subset of health sciences is public health.

WORKPLACES

Information specialists in the health sciences may choose from a variety of workplaces. Some are in corporate settings such as pharmaceutical or cosmetic company libraries. Others work in federally funded organizations such as the National Institutes of Health or Veterans Affairs medical centers. Those based in academic health science libraries may be either privately funded or state funded, depending on the individual institution. Information specialists in academia may serve the health-related disciplines within general universities that offer programs in many areas, or they might work in libraries on health sciences campuses where the libraries concentrate solely on health-related disciplines. Medical research centers employ librarians who can support research in a number of ways, including serving on Institutional Review Boards.

The libraries in these settings can vary greatly in size. In a hospital, there might be only one or two librarians who perform all library functions, whereas in large university libraries the staffs can be quite large and the staff members can each concentrate on particular functions, such as collection development, public access services, reference, website development, user education, or administration. Public libraries provide opportunities for consumer health librarians who assist members of the public by teaching health information literacy and helping them find reliable information in terms that they can understand. Consumer health information librarianship can be very rewarding and can be practiced in hospital or other health care settings, with nonprofit support organizations, and in public libraries. In some institutions, medical librarians are employed by particular clinical departments rather than by libraries. In other cases, medical librarians might be employed by libraries but are embedded in subject-specific departments to serve their information needs. More often, librarians are going to the point where information is needed, rather than waiting for clients to come to them. In a hospital setting, there is sometimes a clinical medical librarian who makes rounds with physicians to search the literature for answers to clinical questions for patient care. Those who have specialized backgrounds in addition to their library science degrees may be called "informationists" or "information specialists" in context.

SPECIAL REQUIREMENTS

So what does one do to become proficient as a health sciences librarian? The MLA has developed competencies for professional success for health sciences librarians in its educational policy statement, "Competencies for Lifelong Learning and Professional Success: The Educational Policy Statement of the Medical Library Association."

Professional Competencies for Health Sciences Librarians

1. Understand the health sciences and health care environment and the policies, issues, and trends that impact that environment.
2. Know and understand the application of leadership, finance, communication, and management theory and techniques.
3. Understand the principles and practices related to providing information services to meet users' needs.
4. Have the ability to manage health information resources in a broad range of formats.

5. Understand and use technology and systems to manage all forms of information.
6. Understand curricular design and instruction and have the ability to teach ways to access, organize, and use information.
7. Understand scientific research methods and have the ability to critically examine and filter research literature from many related disciplines.

Requirements vary from one setting to another and from one position to another. In addition to the master's degree in library or information science, some medical librarians find it helpful to have an undergraduate degree in one of the biological sciences, although such preparation is rarely an absolute prerequisite to employment. There are some librarians who hold graduate degrees in both library science and a health specialty, such as public health, veterinary medicine, or nursing. Some health sciences libraries' position advertisements will express either a requirement or a preference for membership in the Academy of Health Information Professionals (AHIP). AHIP is MLA's peer-reviewed professional development and career recognition program (see "Academy of Health Information Professionals" listed in the References). Although membership in the academy may not be required for a particular position, it can still be helpful for progressing in a career in medical librarianship. Academy membership recognizes the time and effort a health sciences librarian commits to professional development activities and demonstrates academic preparation, as well as professional experience and accomplishments ("Frequently Asked Questions about AHIP"). Membership requires coursework in each of the competencies listed in Professional Competencies for Health Sciences Librarians.

Entry-level positions in health sciences work settings do not require previous experience in a health sciences library. Specialized positions or those with supervisory responsibility will often require a number of years of experience and might or might not specify that the experience be in a health sciences library or some other type of relevant background. In some institutions, the director of an academic health sciences library is encouraged to have a doctorate in an appropriate field. Those in information technology positions in medical libraries might be required to have particular computer-related certifications.

Those working in health-related settings must have or acquire knowledge of specific databases, such as MEDLINE, CINAHL, PsycINFO, Toxnet, and Embase, as well as knowledge of special vocabularies, for example, Medical Subject Headings (MeSH). MEDLINE is a database created at NLM and is free on its PubMed platform. It is also available through a number of proprietary vendor systems that offer different features and search capabilities. The resources used by medical librarians are dynamic. Semantic MEDLINE is a tool that is evolving from MEDLINE and offers a novel path for discovery with the possibility of new roles that librarians can play in research. Rather than simply facilitating the identification of already published research, this tool can actually be used to reveal new discoveries by exploring meaningful relationships that were previously unrealized. Medical librarians should be familiar with the literature and websites of the appropriate disciplines for their work settings.

Health information practitioners should also be familiar with the library requirements for accrediting bodies of their particular institutions. Likewise, they should be conversant with the privacy and confidentiality requirements on medical information that apply to everyone in their workplace, such as the Health Insurance Portability and Accountability Act (HIPAA), and the Human Research Protection Programs (HRPP), in addition to the "Code of Ethics for Health Sciences Librarianship."

How does one obtain the specialized knowledge to be a health sciences librarian? A number of library science schools offer health sciences librarianship courses in their curricula. The American Library Association (ALA) (2014) offers a directory of accredited library schools detailing the specialty tracks that those schools provide, including health sciences librarianship and health informatics. There is a postgraduate certificate program for those who wish to specialize in health sciences librarianship *after* obtaining a library science degree. This information is also included in the ALA directory.

There are scholarships specifically for those who intend to pursue careers in health sciences librarianship, such as the MLA Scholarship for Minority Students, two of the ALA Spectrum Scholarships, which are cosponsored by the NLM and MLA, and the MLA Scholarship. The Thompson/Reuters/MLA Doctoral Fellowship is an opportunity for those wishing to earn doctorates.

For those who already have a library science degree, a number of continuing education courses are available that are pertinent to health sciences settings. These can be useful for health sciences librarians who need to update their skills or learn about new technologies, as well as for practicing librarians who have no previous health science experience but are interested in preparing for the specialty. Continuing education courses are available from a number of professional organizations, such as MLA. The NLM offers free courses through its eight regional programs. Certifications in consumer health information and disaster information are available through a curriculum offered by the MLA and can enhance a professional's qualifications for particular work settings.

While additional education or specialized experience can be required to excel in some health sciences librarianship positions, the extra effort can often be worth it in terms of compensation. Another route to higher compensation is joining AHIP, which correlates with a higher average salary for those certified at the Member, Senior, and Distinguished levels. Only Provisional Academy members, who have less than five years' experience, have lower average salaries than non-AHIP members.

INTERNSHIPS AND WORK EXPERIENCE

Graduate assistantships are often available and provide another means of support while offering experience. Other health sciences opportunities for graduate library science students include unpaid internships, practica, or field experiences for which they can get academic credit. These internships are often in academic health sciences libraries, but are not limited to academic settings. A less formal way to get health sciences library experience is volunteering in institutions that offer volunteer programs. While there is no academic credit or monetary compensation, volunteer experience can help determine whether or not medical librarianship is a good fit for a person. If so, this experience can be added to one's résumé in the future for employment applications in medical libraries and can be a source of references.

For recent library science graduates who are interested in health sciences librarianship as a career, the NLM offers an opportunity to apply for its associate fellowship, which is a one- to two-year residency program on the NLM campus in Bethesda, Maryland. For those who are further along in their career trajectories with some management experience under their belts and an interest in becoming academic health sciences library directors, there is a leadership fellowship program cosponsored by the Association of Academic Health Sciences Libraries and NLM. This program places the fellows with mentors who are experienced directors.

CAREER PATHS

Career paths in health sciences librarianship are variable. Successful medical librarians might start in entry-level positions in academic health sciences libraries, progressing to positions of more responsibility. They might start in one-person government libraries and move to national-level positions in the National Institutes of Health or Department of Veterans Affairs. They might start out in small hospital libraries and move into hospital administration. Conversely, they can move from one type of setting to another. Mobility among different types of health sciences libraries is certainly possible and occurs regularly in the medical librarian population. The career paths are limitless. While solo librarians are generally more likely to move to libraries with larger staffs and set about progressing upward within those staffs, movement is not always in that direction. Librarians in the federal government system, even when working in small libraries, often receive better compensation than their counterparts directing larger staffs. As health sciences librarians' roles evolve and expand to include e-science, management of big data, translational science, continuing medical education, integration of knowledge-based information into electronic health records, patient education, patient health records, and management of research repositories, traditional paths of the past will change somewhat. Emerging roles for medical librarians are described in a special issue of the *Journal of the Medical Library Association* ("New Roles for Health Science Librarians" 2013). If one compares job titles of the past with current job titles for medical librarians, and compares position descriptions, one can see that there are many more options now. There might not be a common path, but what a joy to know how many possibilities there are!

PROFESSIONAL ORGANIZATIONS TO JOIN

Professional organizations are great places to nurture professional growth. Selected websites are listed in Professional Organizations of Interest to Health Sciences Information Professionals.

Professional associations offer a number of membership benefits such as networking, publications, continuing education, educational conferences, leadership opportunities, mentoring opportunities, listservs, and more. The premier organization for health sciences librarians is the MLA. It has regional divisions called chapters, as well as units called sections, which are based on particular subspecialties, e.g., Hospital Libraries, Leadership and Management, Research, Consumer and Patient Health Information, Medical Informatics, and more. For a complete list, see the MLS Sections page: http://www.mlanet.org/p/cm/ld/fid=439. As mentioned earlier, MLA supports professional development through its scholarships, fellowships, continuing education in a variety of formats, and AHIP. Student and introductory membership levels are available at reduced fees.

The Special Libraries Association is of interest to some health sciences librarians. It has a number of relevant divisions, such as Biomedical & Life Sciences; Food, Agriculture & Nutrition; Leadership & Management; Pharmaceutical & Health Technology; and Solo Librarians. Like MLA, it has geographical divisions called chapters, and it has Student Groups.

Informaticians in the health care arena may belong to the American Medical Informatics Association. Along with health sciences librarians, this organization's membership includes physicians and other health care professionals, health information technologists, researchers, educators, scientists, government officials, consultants, and industry professionals—people who apply computer technology to various aspects of health care practice.

The Association for Information Science and Technology (ASIS&T) focuses on research on the use of information. According to its page on Membership, "ASIS&T is the only professional association that bridges the gap between the diverse needs of researchers, developers and end users, and between the challenge and opportunities associated with emerging technologies and applications" ("Membership"). While the organization is not focused solely on health sciences, it has a special interest group on health informatics and a virtual special interest group on bioinformatics ("Special Interest Groups [SIGS]").

The ALA is the largest library organization in the United States and is more general as a whole, but it does have divisions of particular interest to health sciences librarians, depending on their particular roles and where they work. Those working in academic health sciences libraries might wish to join ALA's Association of College and Research Libraries (ACRL). Medical librarians in management positions might be interested in the Library Leadership and Management Association (LLAMA), while collection management and cataloging (metadata) librarians are more likely to be affiliated with ALA's Association for Library Collections & Technical Services (ALCTS). The Reference and

User Services Association (RUSA) of ALA recently revised its "Health and Medical Reference Guidelines" (2015). ALA is also the organization that accredits library science programs.

PROFESSIONAL ORGANIZATIONS OF INTEREST TO HEALTH SCIENCES INFORMATION PROFESSIONALS

American Library Association: http://www.ala.org/
American Medical Informatics Association: http://www.amia.org/
Association for Information Science and Technology: http://www.asist.org/
Medical Library Association: https://www.mlanet.org/
Special Libraries Association: http://www.sla.org/

PUBLICATIONS TO FOLLOW

Medical librarians may be interested in a number of excellent, nonmedically oriented publications, e.g., *Reference Services Review*, *Journal of the American Society for Information Sciences and Technology*, and *College and Research Libraries*, but there are also a number of serials that specifically emphasize the practice of health sciences information. The major publication for librarians in health information settings is the *Journal of the Medical Library Association*, which publishes research and case reports within the field. MLA members receive the journal as a membership benefit, but it is also available as an open-access publication at PubMed Central. The *Journal of Hospital Librarianship* is recommended for health information practitioners in hospital and other clinical care settings. The articles in *Medical Reference Services Quarterly* are relevant to health sciences librarians in many different situations. Of particular help for librarians who search PubMed and other NLM databases is the *NLM Technical Bulletin*, which is freely available at the NLM website. For those dealing with consumers, whether in a public library, hospital, or cancer center, *Journal of Consumer Health on the Internet* is helpful. The *Journal of the American Medical Informatics Association* is pertinent to the work of librarians in health informatics.

Though certainly not in the category of peer-reviewed publications, e-mail discussion lists can be very helpful. A number of listservs are available to medical librarians, the main one being MEDLIB-L, which serves a community of health sciences librarians who help each other with questions and problems. Although the listserv is sponsored by the MLA, being a list participant in MEDLIB-L does not require a paid subscription or membership in a particular organization.

FINAL WORDS

Health sciences librarianship is a fascinating, rewarding field. A health sciences searcher might help save someone's life in the operating room or contribute to grant researchers' work in the discovery of medical breakthroughs. A medical librarian might also teach future physicians how to search the literature and critically appraise what they find so that they can practice evidence-based medicine. People who work closely with their health sciences librarians come to depend on them for their expertise. Being needed and appreciated is gratifying. The field of medical librarianship is rapidly changing and expanding—and certainly never boring.

ADDITIONAL READING

Huber, Jeffrey T., and Susan Swogger. 2014. *Introduction to Reference Sources in the Health Sciences.* Chicago: Neal-Schuman, 2014.

Huber, Jeffrey T., and Feili Tu-Keefner, eds. *Health Librarianship: An Introduction.* Santa Barbara, CA: Libraries Unlimited, 2014.

Wood, M. Sandra, ed. *Health Sciences Librarianship.* Lanham, MD: Rowman & Littlefield, 2014.

Wood, M. Sandra, ed. *Introduction to Health Sciences Librarianship.* New York: Haworth Press, 2008.

REFERENCES

"Academy of Health Information Professionals." Medical Library Association. Accessed January 31, 2015. https://www.mlanet.org/academy/.

American Library Association. Committee on Accreditation. "Library & Information Studies. Directory of Institutions Offering Accredited Master's Programs." 2014. http://www.ala.org/accreditedprograms/sites/ala.org .accreditedprograms/files/content/directory/pdf/LIS_directory_7-2014.pdf.

"Code of Ethics for Health Sciences Librarianship." Medical Library Association. 2010. https://www.mlanet.org/about/ethics.html.

"Competencies for Lifelong Learning and Professional Success: The Educational Policy Statement of the Medical Library Association." Medical Library Association. Accessed January 31, 2015. https://www.mlanet.org/education/policy/ index.html.

"Frequently Asked Questions about AHIP." Medical Library Association Academy of Health Information Professionals. Accessed August 26, 2015. https://www.mlanet.org/academy/acadfaq.html.

"Health and Medical Reference Guidelines." American Library Association. Reference and User Services Association. 2015. http://www.ala.org/rusa/ resources/guidelilnes/guidelinesmedical.

"Join an MLA Section." Medical Library Association. Accessed February 4, 2015. https://www.mlanet.org/community/sections/sections.html.

"Membership." Association for Information Science and Technology. Accessed February 1, 2015. http://www.asis.org/membership.php/.

"New Roles for Health Science Librarians." Special Issue. *Journal of the Medical Library Association* 101, no. 4 (2013).

"Special Interest Groups (SIGs)." Accessed February 1, 2015. http://www.asis .org/SIG/sigs.html.

Part II

15   CHANGING FIELDS WITHIN ACADEMIC AND RESEARCH LIBRARIES

Josiah M. Drewry
University of North Carolina at Chapel Hill

Editor's Note:

Librarians are an intellectually curious group. That's what many of us love about our colleagues and treasure in ourselves. We read widely in fields that interest us; we pursue additional degrees; we learn new languages; we seek out opportunities for travel and growth. These qualities and actions lead some librarians to consider applying for library positions that are quite different than the one they currently hold at some point in their careers.

This chapter's author, Josiah Drewry, shares wisdom based on his own experiences. He has used his impressive skills sets and adaptability to work as a humanities librarian, a generalist, and a business librarian in the United States, Morocco, and Egypt.

In the pages that follow, Drewry focuses on helping librarians who have experience in one specialty area identify and adapt the skills they have built in order to prepare for a very different position. His suggestions will help librarians make a strong case for themselves when they apply for a position. His plan for informing oneself about the programs and individuals that a particular position serves will help a librarian provide the best possible service from the beginning. The chapter conveys a valuable message for all academic librarians whose continually developing expertise leads them down a changing path: experience in a subject area matters, of course, but librarians can make the choice to actively develop that expertise. They can take steps to shape their own successes and to move their careers in new directions. Combining enthusiasm for learning with a commitment to serving patrons well opens up a realm of possibilities for academic librarians who want to keep moving and evolving.

INTRODUCTION

This chapter is written primarily for those starting a new position at a different library or institution, or taking on a new subject specialty without switching employers, or making a much more radical change to a new category of library or organization. It discusses all major job duties that make up the contemporary subject specialist librarian model: collection development and analysis in one or more subject areas; individual or group instruction and reference consultations related to these subject areas; and outreach to faculty, students, affiliated staff, and sometimes populations outside the university. This may also include responsibilities like assisting in data gathering or analysis, or planning workshops or other events in the library. Actual duties and terminologies may vary widely between libraries or between different positions within a single library. The guiding principle of this chapter is that becoming a star subject specialist in a new setting is about recognizing and mastering transferrable skills. Knowledge or skills developed in one position can be deployed in a similar one, perhaps in a different discipline, or even in another language, in another country, at a later time.

GETTING THE JOB

For a subject specialist, a successful job search will require some demonstrated knowledge of one or more academic disciplines. It will also require intellectual flexibility and a good deal of social skill. The first task is to convince a hiring committee that one already has either relevant work experience in the discipline in question or significant insight into how research is conducted and disseminated in that field. Generally, either one will be enough to advance an applicant's candidacy partway, though the successful candidate will likely need both if the position is very competitive.

In some cases, an undergraduate degree in the discipline in question will satisfy the library's "required" or "preferred" qualifications for subject knowledge. However, either direct experience as a subject specialist in the field or a master's degree in a closely related field (demonstrating research skills) will often be given more weight. In other cases, a master's or a PhD in the exact field or related field will be part of the job description, although it is often preferred rather than required. The bar will generally be set higher at larger, more research-oriented institutions, and in libraries dedicated to particular populations or fields of study.

When the hiring committee has determined that a candidate meets the minimum requirements and extends an invitation to interview, then other criteria are considered. Hiring committees want to see evidence that candidates understand what the work flow will be like in this new position, as well as what their strategic and everyday priorities would be, and how they, their patrons, and their supervisor(s) might define success. Interviewers will also look for creativity, enthusiasm, tact, and good judgment, which are all keys to flourishing as a subject specialist.

To prepare for a job interview, a candidate should think very carefully about the key questions he or she will likely be asked related to outreach, collection development, reference, and instruction in an academic discipline. Here are some sample questions from the American Library Association's New Members' Round Table "Academic Interview Process" site:

- What is the most challenging thing you do in your current job?
- What would you tell us about your library collections?
- Are you a self-starter?
- How do you deal with difficult patrons?

Thinking through these and other questions shared on the site can help job candidates think through answers and scenarios that they might use as responses during their own interviews. Spending some time thinking through answers to common interview questions in advance can help interviews go much more smoothly and successfully.

Liaison duties are often defined broadly for hiring purposes. A main library may be looking for a social sciences librarian instead of a psychology librarian, for instance, because the skills used in one social science are generally transferrable to another, or because they anticipate having to shuffle liaison duties in the future. If they find a candidate who possesses a compelling mix of skills but lacks some subject-specific knowledge, a sensible hiring committee may collectively shrug, say "Well, they can learn that . . . ," and then hire them anyway. This is perfectly appropriate, as every major part of a subject liaison's job demands ongoing, active, and self-directed learning. With an open mind, a subject specialist can take full advantage of any task that bestows subject-specific knowledge or special skills upon them.

STARTING THE JOB

It is easy to identify broad characteristics that distinguish one academic field or group of fields from others. In physics or chemistry, for instance, two of the hardest "hard" sciences, research takes place in the laboratory, and modes of inquiry are dictated by the scientific method. There is also observation and experimentation in the social sciences, as well as a heavy focus on statistical analysis of data, but there is more debate in these fields about what constitutes legitimate methods or meaningful results. Qualitative data plays a large role alongside quantitative data. The main subjects of interest in these disciplines are individuals or groups whose behaviors and relationships are complex, constantly evolving, and difficult to measure.

Thus while it is simple to divide disciplines into broad classes, it is less obvious what this means for a librarian switching into a liaison role, or from one subject to another. For example, many humanities librarians would be quite nervous at the prospect of filling in for a librarian in the "hard" (physical or natural) sciences. But advances in the hard sciences depend largely on access to current and recent research, often well organized and easily found in top research journals and open-access repositories. In contrast, humanities and social science librarians deal with a tail of relevant scholarship and potential research materials that is as long as human history, and found in an endless array of languages, sources, and formats.

Here are some more questions to help strategize about becoming a departmental liaison:

- What majors or degrees does the department offer? What minors, certificates, and concentrations?
- What are the major subdisciplines within the department, and are faculty grouped into corresponding units? These units will usually be described on departmental websites.
- Areas of emphasis within the curriculum will dictate at least some priorities in collection development, and reveal some resources and theories that a job applicant might be expected to know.
- Remember that a faculty member's research and teaching may correspond well to subdiscipline or unit boundaries, but often this is not the case. They may also be involved in interdisciplinary or multidisciplinary research.
- How large is the department? How many professors, lecturers, adjuncts, graduate students, and undergraduates? If the department is massive, the liaison might not have the capacity to approach each faculty member or come to every research-oriented class, and will have to prioritize. If the liaison is responsible for multiple departments, then the relative size of each may also be useful in work flow planning.
- Is the department established, evolving, or just getting off the ground? Are there any new majors, minors, or course sequences, either recently established or in the planning stages? Departments of any maturity level may require benchmarking against other departments on campus or at other schools, or assistance with identification of publication opportunities. A well-established department may have one or more "stars" in the field, or a long history of publications in first- and second-tier journals. A new department may need materials that will help support the basics of research that its students and faculty will perform. The department should have well-defined and rigorous criteria for faculty tenure and promotion; look for documents that are germane to library work, such as a list of preferred journals, which would be top priorities for collection development. If the department is large enough, it may even host its own journal or depository in-house.

- Are there any entities that are applying for accreditation or are up for review? The liaison may be asked to buy materials or develop a collection development policy to support these, or assist in gathering information and writing documents for accreditation. New programs or initiatives are also a good opportunity for outreach and collaboration with faculty or another subject liaison.

Think about who in the library or in other groups across campus may have a role that is naturally complementary to the subject specialist's. At a larger college or university, there will probably be many: other librarians, instructional technologists, departmental researchers, graduate research assistants and teaching assistants, grant-funded employees, and others. Once key contacts are identified, talking to them can reveal where collaboration is welcome, and where it is not. This process helps to avoid confrontation and duplication of effort. It might also provide some willing partners with valuable institutional memory and unique perspectives. They can act as a sounding board for ideas, and can facilitate introductions to high-value outreach targets.

COLLECTIONS AND THE DISCIPLINES

When switching fields, it is useful to compare the curricula vitae (CVs) and citation counts of a few faculty members in new field with some from other fields, matching them by status or years of experience if possible. See what they publish, where their data come from, and what kinds of materials they cite most often. Many disciplines, especially in the sciences, will use open-access journals and repositories when possible, because timeliness is paramount, research teams may be distributed globally, and they may have the financial resources to self-publish. In other disciplines, scholarly monographs and traditional journal content remains the norm.

Each different field will have distinct patterns of scholarly communications, so continue to be mindful of the differences in research output and collection use between fields. Liaisons to one field may spend 90 percent or more of the collections budget on scholarly journals, while others collect heavily in several formats. In some fields or subfields, there may be only one or two "core" journal packages or other resources, while others may be covered only by a broad range of sources and formats.

The collection development duties required in a new position may be intimidating, especially if one takes a position in a new library with a totally different working culture, patron base, and budgetary idiosyncrasies. However, collection assessment skills are often easily transferrable from one position to another. There are a number of tools to help librarians assess usage of or "holes" in their collections, including OCLC's Worldcat Collection Analysis, in-house circulation reports, other library collections close by, consortial usage statistics, interlibrary borrowing statistics, "turnaway" statistics from unsubscribed database content, course reading lists, and analysis of CVs and recent papers and presentations.

Liaisons must make sure they understand the basic factors affecting their spending on materials. If they are collecting for a department at the PhD level, instead of the master's or bachelor's level, they will need to collect and retain core titles, as well as a range of sources that may be of interest only to a handful of researchers in the field or subfield. Below-average usage across these specialized sources may be acceptable, as long as important emerging research needs of departmental faculty and graduate students are being met. Most libraries have approval plans in place that will address these needs automatically, and many services have arisen over the years to address the inherent uncertainty of collecting on a limited budget, including interlibrary loan, demand-driven acquisitions, and even the classic purchase request form. Even the best liaisons will never be able to predict usage on a title-by-title basis, nor will they be able to guess which specialized data sets faculty or graduate students will need before they need them.

Besides contacts in a liaison's "official" department or departments, many librarians will keep a list of research centers and other constituencies on and off campus that may depend on the collections they build. Many of these people will likely come to the subject specialist sooner or later with research needs, and it could be fruitful to approach some of them first. They might have funding of their own that they can contribute toward richer research collections; it is often worthwhile to ask.

The same principle applies if the needs of a liaison's departments are very multidisciplinary. If they are, there are usually many opportunities to collaborate with other liaisons in related fields. Most commonly, liaisons will look out for material that might interest each other's constituents, and talk about pooling funds to purchase materials with obvious interdisciplinary appeal.

As this book is published, and for at least a few more years, libraries will wrestle with how to choose between print books and e-books containing the same content. E-books are searchable, they don't go missing, and they are often available to multiple users simultaneously. However, each e-book provider has its own particular usage restrictions, or a range of prices for different levels of restrictiveness. Publishers, aggregators, and even authors change their business models regularly, and a good deal may be here one day and gone the next. Cost and ease of use will factor heavily into a library's purchase decisions, and each library will likely find a range of opinions among its patrons. It can be misleading to make collection decisions based on usage comparisons between print and e-books, however. Librarians often receive more usage statistics with e-books and other databases than are possible with print books, including number of times accessed, downloads, user sessions, page views, searches, and more. While these statistics can be useful for demonstrating value with precision, they should not be weighted exactly the same as the circulation statistics that are available for print books or serials. For instance, how many times has a print book been taken off the shelf, examined, and then reshelved without being checked out?

Most libraries have no idea. How many print pages have been scanned, by either eyeballs or an actual scanner? There is no good way to tell.

Finally, when librarians switch to a new position, they will likely have to update their list of vendor contacts, or build it from scratch. Moving into business librarianship or another field with expensive and highly competitive data providers, librarians will get more unsolicited calls and e-mails from vendors than they did before. The same may also be true when moving from a small institution to a large institution or one that is perceived to have a lot of money. For a new liaison, developing good relationships with multiple vendors can help in assessing the landscape of available products and potential research needs. It is always good to know what new products are on the market, and if they are worth pursuing. Most subject specialists will have a list of resources that they would buy if they had more money, and many will know what they would cut first in the event of an acute budget shortfall. If subject specialists have strong partnerships with vendors, their libraries may be offered special discounts, opportunities to help shape a product, or other benefits they might otherwise not receive.

REFERENCE AND INSTRUCTION

The biggest differences between an old position and a new one may be found in the classroom or in research consultations with new patrons. Many subject specialists have built up their instruction skills in a "generalist" instruction or reference role or as a liaison in another discipline; they may need to apply only the skills they already have to a discipline that may be new to them. Answers to the following questions will depend on the size, style, and mission of the college or university, but they will affect how the subject specialist structures lesson plans and builds relationships.

- What groups have significant teaching roles? Professors, adjuncts, or graduate students? Are there professors of practice who aren't expected to perform research? In contrast, are there research professors that won't be found in the classroom? If there are distinct groups, then outreach strategies can be more tailored to each. Maybe a research professor can be found more often at his or her second office in a research center on campus, or maybe the graduate student has a carrel in the library instead of an office within the department.
- Are there a large number of classes that are crosslisted with other disciplines? These might be good opportunities to team up with another subject specialist in the classroom.
- Are there many online classes or night classes? If so, it may be especially worthwhile to make contact with people that teach them, since the liaison is less likely to see them or their students on campus. Online research guides or tutorials can be especially helpful here.
- Is this a discipline that requires a lot of writing and research from undergraduates, or is research and discussion primarily reserved for graduate

students and faculty? If it is the latter, then the liaison to that department might spend less time in the classroom than their peers, but perhaps more time working individually with graduate students.

Some faculty will seek out their departmental liaison and schedule instruction sessions far in advance. If a subject specialist is new in their role, they should first focus on providing some continuity. One way to do this is to spend some time looking at whatever instruction statistics their department has kept, going back three to five years. In most cases, the classes one's predecessor has taught for will still contain research components. Looking up who is teaching these classes next semester to see if they would like to schedule an instruction session may be the perfect opening for longer-term outreach efforts.

The next step is to identify other classes in the department that require significant library research. This means looking through recent course syllabi, which one can usually find on faculty web pages, posted on the campus learning management system, by Googling the class numbers, or by asking departmental administrators. Class syllabi and their associated assignments can be very helpful in planning and assessing a librarian's own work. These discuss key sources and how they are used, and may hint at the tone and structure of the class and the personality and expectations of the instructor.

Each new discipline presents different types of class projects and entire methods of teaching and organizing classes that may seem new. Some disciplines expect undergraduates to perform their own research from the first month of freshman year, while others require only exams for most of the curriculum. Experiential learning, often involving community partnerships or internships, is more and more common in a number of disciplines. In some graduate or upper-level undergraduate courses, replication studies are common, in which students need to run a study using the exact data (or similar data) that other scholars have already used in their research.

More and more faculty are seeing the benefits of the "flipped" classroom model, or entire semesters of role-playing, where students use primary sources to inform their inhabited roles, their writing assignments, or their debates with other students. It may take time to figure out how to add value in these settings. On the other hand, librarians can be a force in helping their new discipline evolve, especially if they apply what they have learned from observing teaching methods elsewhere.

If they have an instruction session planned for a class, some librarians will ask to sit in at other times. This is a sneaky way to lead students to the library and learn more about their needs. Going the week before the instruction session can help in learning what to do and not do. Going the week after can help in connecting with students further. Even if liaisons are very knowledgeable about their field, it may have been years since they have sat in classes, and they may have forgotten what teaching techniques used to work or not work on them. They can learn how to tweak their teaching style or content to provide more continuity for students, or to fill in gaps that are obviously missing.

Reference statistics from the recent past will also be useful to view alongside instruction statistics. Detailed notes will help identify patterns in reference queries, and some good resources to help respond to them. Predecessors may have had a large number of reference questions from certain people or groups of people, on and off campus, and perusing these statistics carefully is a good way to identify these groups and anticipate their needs.

MORE ABOUT OUTREACH

Switching fields means leaving behind a known and often comfortable quantity, and setting aside much of the knowledge and status that one has built up over time. Newness isn't entirely a disadvantage, though. Asking for help or information is a time-tested way to establish relationships.

Soon enough, the new person will have to be the expert again, and outreach duties demand that they have answers. Branding oneself is a part of outreach, and a subject specialist should work to brand themselves before their patrons collectively do it for them. A liaison's brand, their expertise, and the full sum of the library's collections, services and spaces, are actually all parts of one product that the liaison is "selling" through outreach. As the most important link between the library and its regular users, the liaison is also the PR expert, and the front-line customer service representative when the product breaks or when the customer doesn't understand how to use it.

To library patrons, this product is usually free. This means that many will never recognize its true value. The product can also be difficult to use, and faces major competition, from the free web and other places. In many outreach-related scenarios, the subject specialist may be the only one in the room who knows how valuable this product is, and how expensive it is to produce and maintain. It is up to the subject specialist's own expertise and communications skills to unlock the library's value for patrons. Luckily, some of the target population will actually start spreading the message among their peers. These are often called "champions," and they can be found anywhere; sometimes their usefulness is magnified by being in positions of power and trust. There won't be many of them, but luckily, only a few are needed. Ask them for help, and they will happily help demonstrate the library's value to others, often with more authority and insight than even the best subject specialist.

Unfortunately, many of those among a subject specialist's target population are indifferent to the services they provide, while others are very difficult to please. This is true across disciplines. However, those that never respond to advances are often just busy. They may have dual appointments, or be on a number of committees and task forces. On the other hand, they may be lovely people and quite responsive in person, and one may learn a lot from a precious few minutes with them. If an e-mail or a phone call isn't enough, a knock on an office door or an introduction at a seminar or social event might work surprisingly well.

For help with contacting faculty members, many liaisons turn to departmental administrative assistants, who know how research is performed in the discipline, and who know personally (and oversee the schedules of) many prime outreach targets. Administrative assistants will often add librarians directly to a departmental listserv, or at least forward announcements to people they know will be interested. They may also know far in advance who will be taking a sabbatical next semester, or who is never in their office, or who has an interesting project that they might need help with.

Graduate research assistants can also help demonstrate the library's value to faculty. These students may also be performing significant research on their own and need a librarian's help. Graduate students who are teaching are another population that is ripe for outreach, since some of them will be closer to their students (and other graduate students) than professors are. Many of them are also teaching for the first time, and will be grateful for any help. Finally, if they have time, many subject specialists look into undergraduate clubs and other events. If there are groups whose missions are in some way related to a librarian's disciplines, they may appreciate help in organizing an event or a public service campaign. Leaders of student organizations can be valuable and credible champions for the library as a whole.

TIPS FOR GETTING UP TO SPEED

Librarians who know in advance that they are switching fields can make good use of the time they have by doing the following:

- Reading some recent journal articles by their future faculty members, or at least reading some abstracts and literature reviews
- Reading one of the "Very Short Introduction" series, or a classic text in the field
- Browsing textbooks and required reading at the campus bookstore, or browsing the shelves at a "real" bookstore
- Scouring campus newspapers and magazines for mentions of the new department, interviews with new faculty, or examples of award-winning student projects

Subject specialists will be in a hurry to familiarize themselves with the most important sources in their new field, which will likely be major database platforms. Familiarity with these is critical, but some liaisons tend to forget about or ignore the print sources in their discipline, even if they used them heavily in another job or in school. This means they will be ignorant of some key sources, especially if they began their career in a world no longer dominated by print. For sources that weren't born digital, looking at the print predecessor can help make more sense of the electronic version.

Along with syllabi, subject specialists will also learn by reading faculty CVs from time to time. Why? Librarians might get to spend an hour or two with a class that meets for an entire semester, or five minutes with a certain faculty member while several students are waiting outside her office. Reading syllabi and CVs helps keep librarians up to date with the most relevant subject knowledge and armed with other information that is useful for instruction, outreach, and collections duties.

Reading faculty blogs, personal websites, interviews, and other less formal communications is often the best way to learn what faculty are most passionate about in their work or their personal lives. It also helps to develop additional dimensions or layers of depth in librarian-faculty relationships. Any kind of "lead" helps establish the librarian as someone who is doing more than just taking up precious time.

Recent formal assessments like LibQual, surveys through Ithaka S+R, and others can prove tremendously useful in comparing different disciplines or academic departments. Internally published reports from these assessments should contain aggregated survey data about library use and research patterns, by school, by department, and sometimes by demographic. They should also include selected comments from students, faculty, and staff about collections and services that liaisons help provide.

If a break from reading is needed, there may be a number of massive online open courses (often referred to as "MOOCs") aimed at the subject specialist's core constituency, or videos from YouTube or Khan Academy, or recorded lectures or presentations by star researchers hosted elsewhere. Recent or classic documentaries or other films may also be useful in many disciplines. Librarians are generally not expected to have a PhD-level understanding of their field, but they will need to demonstrate more than a passing notion. How to build this knowledge base is up to the individual.

Many librarians subscribe to regular alerts through Google, Web of Science, Scopus, or other databases, which can help track faculty publications or new trends in research. However, these will not provide a cohesive understanding of the field, and because of how much time it takes to publish a paper, will usually not reveal what a researcher is working on at the moment. To stay current, keep talking to faculty or reading their blogs, and look for the "current research" sections of their CVs or websites.

Be sure to actively seek out relevant e-mail lists and event calendars for assigned departments and related centers on campus. Don't miss out, at least at first. One of the hardest parts of starting a new position is not knowing what information can be safely ignored.

Finally, it is enormously helpful to reach out more to fellow librarians in the field, before and after a transition. Most of us do this, but not nearly enough. This can include attending conferences or being active in subject-oriented groups at the regional or national level, many of which are covered elsewhere in this book. Often, librarians find even greater value in local professional organizations or consortial groups, or national/international subject-oriented listservs. As well as connecting subject specialists with experts in real time, professional groups and listservs often have searchable archives that go back years, which can help answer common questions.

TIPS FOR SLOWING DOWN

After starting a new job and settling in, some subject specialists will continue to look for important e-mail lists, calendars, and events across campus. It is OK to ignore these if they're not of central importance. Getting up to speed is NOT about getting pulled in every direction at once. Once a librarian is in a new position, many of their colleagues and most of their patrons will treat them as an expert automatically, even if they don't feel any smarter upon waking than they did the night before. A good liaison will gain motivation directly from the confidence that others have in them.

Most subject specialists are curious, conscientious professionals, and many have cultivated a reputation to match. The most successful ones leave themselves enough time to prepare properly for instruction, research consultations, and outreach. Even if they have had time to build a positive reputation, one bad move, like an unprepared visit to a classroom, can do lasting damage. Experienced subject specialists will avoid putting themselves in such positions by declining when a professor invites them to a class session with too little notice, or when she says, "Oh, I'm sure whatever you come up with will be fine."

A slow and steady increase in workload is ideal, led by outreach strategies and tactics, but not propelled by them. For most subject specialists, meeting or exceeding expectations becomes increasingly difficult as their reputation begins to precede them, as the number and depth of their regular contacts grow, and as committees and noncore demands on their time proliferate. While many are happy to be needed, they may soon wish they had more time to focus on the duties that drew them to the job in the first place. A canny librarian will focus only on the relationships to which they can truly devote their time and energy.

No experienced colleague or supervisor will expect a new subject specialist to know everyone and be everywhere immediately. The most important things a librarian can bring to a new position are a capacity for self-directed learning and a passion for nurturing relationships. The star subject specialists will be the only ones who really know what it takes to do their job well.

REFERENCE

"Academic Interview Process." American Library Association New Members' Round Table. Accessed September 18, 2015. http://www.ala.org/nmrt/oversightgroups/comm/resreview/process

16 PREPARING TO MOVE UP THE LADDER

Lisa Norberg
K | N Consultants

Editor's Note:

Throughout this chapter, Lisa Norberg mentions the value of seeking out mentorship from trusted colleagues. Lisa herself has been a friend and the most skillful of mentors to me for over 10 years. One of the aspects of her mentoring that I most appreciate formed a major theme in this chapter: her belief that "moving up" means moving toward one's own career goals, whatever they may be. For some librarians, that means progressing higher into the ranks of library administration. For many others, it may mean finding a job at a library with a great collection in their field, getting to work with materials in a language they speak, or taking a position where they'll be able to help shape a new service or learning space. Some librarians have an ultimate career goal in mind: they know what title they hope to hold when they retire. Others want to keep themselves engaged with fresh opportunities and material and see where the path leads them.

Lisa discusses preparation for "moving up" in two basic scenarios: how librarians can take advantage of opportunities to grow in their current positions, and how they can select new jobs wisely. By continually excelling and selectively taking on new responsibilities, they can always be in a state of moving forward, no matter what their current job situation. Her chapter provides concrete suggestions as well as hope.

MY OWN CAREER PATH

For close to a quarter of a century, I have worked in a variety of library positions in different sizes and types of institutions—from subject liaison to coordinator of instruction, from director of public services to dean, and now to the principal of a nonprofit organization. It might appear like a well-planned progressive journey. It was not. I discovered that advancing my career was subject to a range of forces—politics, relationships, timing, and chance—that were beyond my span of control. What I did have along the way was a number of amazing people who mentored and guided me. With this chapter, I hope to share some of my own experiences and insights, along with some of the wisdom that was shared with me.

My career in libraries began literally by accident. I did not spring from my mother's womb knowing I wanted to be a librarian. I did not grow up going to the public library every Saturday. I did not classify my childhood book collection. I was not an English major. I went to graduate school to become a bureaucrat—a high-minded socially and environmentally sensitive one, to be sure—but a bureaucrat nonetheless. My career began with a scheduling error. I was in my first semester of graduate school when I accidently enrolled in a library science course I mistakenly thought was a computer course. That twist of fate that set me off on a completely different career path was sealed not by the riveting content of the library science class (with no offense to the truly wonderful professor who taught the class), but the number of incredibly generous and funny classmates who would later be my colleagues. When I discovered I could pair my interest in public affairs with librarianship and work with people like this, I was hooked.

My first professional position out of library school was as a liaison librarian with a subject specialization in public and international affairs. I was thrilled. As a subject specialist, I audited classes and asked faculty to share their syllabi so I could better understand the information needs of their students; I studied the curricula vitae of faculty so I would be familiar with their areas of research and could build our collections to support it; I browsed the table of contents of key journals and familiarized myself with the leading publishers and presses in the field; I mastered the specialized resources and tools used by researchers; I followed important scholars in the field and networked with other subject specialists. I did many of the same things my coauthors suggest in this book, only in that pre-Google, ProQuest, pre-Twitter sort of way. I loved being a subject specialist and I took enormous pride doing what I could to facilitate the research and education of the students and faculty with whom I worked. The occasional thank-you note from a student or reference from one faculty member to another was and both gratifying and motivating. I knew what it took to be a good subject specialist, and any time responsibilities shifted and I was asked to take on a new subject, I was confident I knew the steps necessary to meet the requirements of the job.

My next position confirmed my ability to expand my expertise, but it also gave me an opportunity to begin to develop a new set of skills. I was still a subject specialist, but had broadened my responsibilities to include government information. While government information had always been an important element in my work as a subject specialist, my new role gave me the opportunity to delve further into the diverse array of government information resources and the variety of ways different researchers and scholars approach and use the information.

Instead of just knowing how a bill becomes a law, the best source for presidential campaign finance reports, or how to Shepardize a court case, I needed to know how to export economic data from the Federal Reserve for students and faculty from business and economics and import climate data into geographic information systems (commonly referred to as "GIS") for students and faculty from agriculture and environmental sciences. Aside from the fact that this has all become a whole lot easier, the experience exposed me to new technologies and research methods I had not known previously. It gave me a broader perspective on the needs of different disciplines and a better sense of the role the library could play in the academic enterprise.

During this time, I found that sharing my newfound knowledge and skills with others was incredibly rewarding. I developed an interest in library instruction and looked for ways to enhance my teaching style, including enrolling in a master's program in training and development. I was well into my new degree program when a job announcement caught my eye. The position was coordinator of instruction services. I must confess, I was naïve to the notion that positions with "coordinator" in the title are a recipe for failure—"all the responsibility, none of the authority"—so I pressed on oblivious to the challenges that come with bringing people together to make something happen. Little did I know that this would be one of the most transformative experiences I would have in my career. It taught me how to pull together a diverse team of people with a mix of technical skills, content knowledge, teaching experience, and novel ideas, and motivate them to work together to achieve a common objective. Along the way, I learned the importance of not only understanding but also appreciating and accepting the unique culture of a library, a campus, and a region. I learned to value the contributions that individuals with unique skills and distinct personalities could bring to an endeavor.

I was fortunate at this time to also begin teaching as an adjunct professor in a school of library and information science. I discovered that leading a class was not unlike leading a project. Communication was key. I needed to find a way to convey a concept in ways that individuals from different backgrounds with varying levels of interest and motivation could follow and understand. Each class had a unique culture, the combination of a range of skills and personalities, and each represented a snapshot of time in the profession. The experience reinforced my passion for teaching, but also taught me the vital role mentorship plays in the profession. For the first time in my career, a group of people looked to me for guidance as I had looked to others. At the same time I was becoming aware of my own influence, I also began to recognize the immense gratification that comes from helping others succeed.

Then I got lucky. Following a handful of retirements and resignations, the library director reorganized and the position of director of public services was created. I turned to my colleagues and mentors for advice and all convinced me it would be a good move professionally and encouraged me to apply. After securing the position, I quickly realized that I needed to acquire a new set of skills, as well as to hone the ones I had. I had gone from supervising one librarian and a handful of students to overseeing numerous core library services, including circulation, research, instruction, and interlibrary loan. And the same organizational change that had worked to my advantage was not embraced with the same positive enthusiasm by all those affected.

My education in managing people commenced. I discovered that my sense of having more authority was more illusion than reality. Middle management may have carried with it more responsibility, but it required the same ability to bring people together to achieve a common goal that my job as coordinator had. As a middle manager, I learned how to communicate up, over, and across. I learned what it meant to have someone's back and to stand on principle. I learned to trust and empower rather than to doubt or assume. This period of my career was punctuated by a series of successes and failures—some big, some small—but all of which contained valuable lessons in the core elements of management and leadership and prepared me for my next move.

A life change brought with it the need to relocate and another opportunity to advance. It didn't happen overnight, but I eventually found a position that was in many ways ideal. I became the dean of a small liberal arts college library closely associated with a major research university and library system. In addition to the library, the position was also responsible for classroom and instructional technology so that ability to understand a different culture and master new subject matter once again proved invaluable. This time, however, I was the one to initiate much needed, but deeply resisted organizational change. Urged on and supported by the college administration, we went through two difficult reorganizations, revising job descriptions, cutting and merging positions, and creating new ones. It was painful for everyone involved and I quickly learned what it means to be "lonely at the top." It took courage and integrity to reposition and replace, yet, after those first painful months past, we turned a corner and began to see the benefits of our transformation. Faculty who had long written off both the library and our instructional support suddenly discovered they could not only depend on us to provide the services they needed, but partner with us to launch exciting new instructional initiatives. To keep up with the ever-evolving teaching, research, and information environment, we developed a culture that was dynamic and innovative, characterized by respect, wonder, and delight. Work was fun.

Then circumstances changed. My boss left, and after a year and a half with an interim supervisor, my new boss was hired. At the same time, plans were under way to design and build a new building, which would house a new state-of-the-art library. After years spent building a twenty-first-century organization, I was excited to participate in a building project that would match the organization's newfound skills and ambition. Early in the planning process, however, it became clear that the university administration's objectives did not align with ours. I found myself unable to advocate effectively on behalf of my staff with my own professional knowledge and experience disregarded. I realized that despite being at the "top" of the org chart, I had very little control over other agendas.

The situation became increasingly dysfunctional and I knew the best thing I could do was leave. So I did.

I was fortunate in that I had a Plan B. For several years, I had been working nights and weekends with a colleague on a plan for open-access (OA) publishing. As the OA movement was gaining traction, we were urged by a number of people to stop talking about our plan and do something about it, so we had established a nonprofit organization. Just after we received our notification from the IRS that they had approved our status as a 501(c)(3) charitable organization, I resigned my position. Unfortunately, the announcement of my resignation was followed by the announcement of the administration's plans for the building and the new library, which upset some members of the faculty. My departure suddenly became entangled in a very public debate over the new building and the future of the library. It was certainly not how I had intended to leave the college or launch my new venture, but it did confirm that I was making the right decision.

My experience at the helm of a not-for-profit organization specializing in OA publishing strategies is too brief to draw many lessons from, but I can report that many of the core skills and values that I applied to previous positions continue to help and guide me. Our major project is the establishment of the Open Access Network (OAN), a scalable and sustainable model of OA publishing and preservation in the humanities and social sciences. Our true aim is to help libraries and other mission-drive organizations make the research and scholarship that is produced by institutions of higher education widely available—not just today, but for future generations. I miss the day-to-day contact I had with my many brilliant and generous colleagues, students, and faculty, but I am enjoying this latest challenge in what continues to be an intellectually stimulating and meaningful career.

DEFINING "UP"

Since we have titled this chapter "Preparing to Move Up the Ladder," we should probably start by defining what we mean by "up." No two careers are alike. Your unique situation and priorities will shape many of the decisions you make along the way. Not everyone's ladder is vertical and there is no singular path to success, however you might define it. To create a meaningful career, you need to think deeply about what you want and what matters most. For many, the position of subject specialist or liaison is intellectually stimulating and completely satisfying. Expanding your expertise through the acquisition of a new language or the mastery of a new tool, and finding new ways to serve scholars and researchers scratches your professional itch. You can stop reading now or hang in there for a few tips that will help you be more effective in the workplace, even if you have no desire to move up. For the rest of you, like me, you may find your interests shift, circumstances change, or you simply want a new challenge. Having the self-awareness to know what your strengths and weaknesses are—your talents, skills, and passions—is critical to knowing what the right next step might be.

If you define "up" as it is most commonly defined in libraries and other organizations, up usually entails assuming a supervisory or management role. As your control extends over larger and larger teams, and eventually entire departments, you ascend the library or organization's hierarchy. Advancement—in terms of title, pay, and recognition—is inextricably tied to your ability to manage people. People management, however, is a specific skill set. Not everyone has it. Not everyone wants to develop it. And sometimes you just don't know if you have it or you don't until you try. Some of you may have the self-awareness to know that a higher-level management position is not for you and some of you will discover that along the way. There are many individuals who move into management only to find they are ill-suited for the role. Once there, they feel trapped, assuming any subsequent move in a direction other than further up is equivalent to failure. This situation happens all too often and causes nothing but grief for the individual and the organization. That said, it is also not uncommon to encounter an organization that has a truly toxic managerial culture. If you find yourself in an academic library or institution that tolerates incompetence or inappropriate work behavior, or otherwise discourages commonsense management practices, realize that it is not you; it's them. The ability to understand when a position or an organization isn't the right fit and the confidence to acknowledge it and make a change is commendable. I don't mean to scare you. Managing people is also an important and rewarding endeavor. Moving up also affords you a seat at the table—it gives you a greater voice in moving the library or organization forward. It is important and we need people willing to take on those challenges.

If moving "up" remains the goal, it is equally important to understand that there is no single surefire path. If you look at the organization chart used by most libraries, you will see that classic well-defined hierarchical structure. The lone box at the top—the pinnacle—represents for many the end goal. The route to the top appears to be clearly marked by boxes designating positions of increasing of authority and responsibility. The path appears straightforward. You start as a subject specialist with a relatively narrow set of responsibilities, but with an eye toward eventually overseeing a group of subject specialists or perhaps a department. Once there, depending on the size of the organization, the next stop might be an assistant or associate position overseeing several departments. Finally, the top box is within reach. Or not . . . .

Today more than ever, libraries are constantly evolving organizations. Hierarchies are flattened, departments are restructured, and positions are merged, moved, and redefined. If there ever was a conventional path to the top, it is not as straightforward as it once was. Unexpected opportunities can open while predicted ones may never. Often a sideways move that exposes you to a different part of the organization or enables you to gain new skills or a different perspective may end up serving you better in the end. It is also useful to keep in mind that it is not always at the top where people make the biggest difference or have the greatest impact. And the more traditional your career path is, the less likely you are to have new ideas or a different perspective to offer a future supervisor or employer. Don't be afraid to mix it up a little.

DO YOUR JOB WELL

So what is within your control? How can you prepare yourself so when the right opportunity opens up you are ready? You can start by doing your current job well. That may seem like an obvious statement, but I have seen a lot of smart, talented, and ambitious colleagues jeopardize their future by failing to follow through on their current assignments. Don't get ahead of yourself. If you are constantly plotting or maneuvering for your next position, you inevitably lose focus on the tasks at hand. Not only will your poor performance frustrate your colleagues, it will aggravate your supervisor, who could prove to be your best ally or your worst enemy when a new opportunity arises. Take some time to establish your credibility and strengthen and nurture relationships with colleagues. Be the person in your organization others can trust to get the job done.

If you have reached that point when your current position no longer challenges you or your day-to-day tasks seem rote, be proactive. Talk to your supervisor about new assignments or projects you can help with or expanding the scope of your job, but don't expect too much. There are a number of completely legitimate reasons why your supervisor may not be able to help you. If they are able to expand your role in some way, be grateful and deliver on whatever new assignments you've taken on. Keep in mind that new projects or responsibilities don't automatically translate into greater authority or more pay. Consider it an investment that will pay off down the road. You don't want to be taken advantage of, but if you have asked for additional work, it isn't fair to resent your manager if they provide those opportunities. Also be mindful not to ask for additional work that you can't handle or that will take away from your existing responsibilities. Balance your ambitions with the other important elements of your life. Ultimately, doing your job well matters.

COP AN ATTITUDE

Demonstrating competence and a strong work ethic go a long way in setting the stage for your next position, but there are a number of other more subtle qualities that are equally, if not more important to develop. At the top of that list is attitude. Never underestimate the power of a positive attitude in the workplace. It may sound cliché, but think about it. Who do you prefer to work with—the colleague with the cranky disposition who is constantly whining about the workload or the colleague who is upbeat and enthusiastic about tackling a new assignment? Too Pollyanna? That's fair. What about the colleagues who are self-deprecating or able to lighten a tense situation with a clever observation or amusing anecdote? I am not suggesting you take on a new persona or try to be someone you are not. It is often enough to let the genuine passion and enthusiasm you have for your work show. Not only should you be cognizant of your tone of voice, your gestures, and your expressions, but lighten up every now and then. Smile, laugh, have a little fun. A positive attitude is powerfully addictive. Not only are people naturally drawn to people who are pleasant or fun to be around, they are more apt to respect and follow their lead. I don't mean to suggest you should always be the life of the party; there are certainly times when humor is better checked at the door. The point is, your ability not only to work collaboratively or get along with your coworkers, but to motivate and inspire them is an essential skill you can begin to hone regardless of where you sit on the org chart.

PLAY WELL WITH OTHERS

In most libraries and organizations, there is no shortage of group work. It may come in the form of a task force, a committee, a team, or just an informal group of colleagues who need to collaborate to get something done. Take a look at some recent job listings and you will probably see something like this: "Ability to work collaboratively in a team environment" or this: "Excellent interpersonal skills, flexibility, and the ability to work independently as well as collaboratively with a variety of project stakeholders." Rather than approaching group work with the usual dread, look at it as an opportunity for professional development.

Regardless of the where you are in the organization or what kind of group it is, being part of a collaborative effort gives you a chance to develop those invaluable interpersonal skills. It can also serve as a platform for showcasing your problem-solving abilities and your capacity for leadership. It took me a while to really comprehend how different committees and task forces operated because each one is unique. You have to start by understanding the purpose of the group and assessing the group dynamics. Who is there and why? Presumably, you were all brought together because you each have some level of expertise, skill, experience, or perspective needed to achieve a particular objective. Try to discern the designated role of your team members, including yourself. Sometimes both the end goal and your role are obvious or made explicit, while other times you may need to ask for clarification.

In formal group settings, there is often a designated leader. He or she may be the person with the most seniority, the one with responsibility for the end product, or the person with a skill set that is key to the project. It could be you. But it might not. If you are not the designated leader, consider offering to take notes for the group. I must confess, for a long time I hated taking minutes in meetings. But over the years, I have learned the value of note taking. First, offering to take notes scores you some serious karma with your colleagues. Moreover, taking notes forces you to listen—to everyone. You pay attention, you ask questions, and you give people the chance to repeat their statements so you are sure you record their thoughts accurately. You may bring welcomed clarity to a discussion. That never hurts. You also gain new insights into the dynamics of the group.

Understanding each individual's viewpoint enables you to sympathize with a colleague who is at odds with the rest of the group. It allows you to appreciate when one of your team members is frustrated with the pace of progress. Knowing what is behind resistance or frustration helps you tackle the problem from another angle or look for a more constructive solution. Showing empathy and removing obstacles facilitate the group's success and are key leadership qualities you can demonstrate regardless of whether or not you are the designated team leader. The idea that only people with authority or in a position of power can make things happen is simply not true. The bottom line is that your ability to work constructively with your colleagues to achieve a goal is critical to moving up the ladder.

FEAR NO DATA

If you want to become a manager or administrator, you need to understand and be able to translate the functional requirements of an operation or service into the appropriate financial requirements. Librarians generally hate to think of libraries as a business. Many, including myself, dislike the term "customer" when referring to library users, patrons, students, or faculty. But services and resources cost and we do have an obligation to the organization or institution we operate within to be fiscally responsible—to make wise decisions with the resources we are given. Often subject specialists are given some percentage of the collection budget to spend on resources and we do our best to spend those funds wisely and on materials we believe will be serve current as well as future students, scholars, and researchers. We typically find it useful to collect data on the circulation, downloads, or other metrics used to assess the use of those materials. We also collect data on the services we offer, the guides we create, and the students and faculty we serve. One important element we often fail to collect data on is our performance or those we supervise. Keep in mind that there are human resources behind the services and resources we provide, and performance assessment is a critical factor in our ability to move the organization forward and to achieve our goals. And finally, remember that it is not enough to simply collect data. We need to analyze, compare, summarize, draw conclusions, and then act on it. As you prepare to move up the ladder know that those skills are essential. Look for opportunities to cultivate and demonstrate them.

KNOW THE (HR)ULES

While we are on the topic of budgets, data, and decision making, let's toss in another subject that rates right up there for sheer entertainment value—human resources (HR). Most of us pay precious little attention to the employee handbook once we have figured out which health plan to choose and how many vacation days we can carry over into the next year; however, understanding the policies, rules, and regulations that govern many of the operations and interactions that take place in an organization can give you valuable insight into how things work and facilitate your ability to get things done. Remember, even if you don't supervise anyone now, there is a good chance that eventually you will. One of the best ways to get a general sense of the HR framework the organization operates under is to look at the process needed to hire someone. It may require a detailed justification, budget impact assessment, space or office planning, a fair and equitable search process, a diverse pool of candidates, interview process, negotiation, background check, and so on. Much of the process may depend on whether the institution is public or private, whether staff are part of a union, or have faculty or administrative status, but the process may also be based on institutional conventions. Presumably, when you were hired you experienced that process from the potential hire angle. Serving on a search committee will give you the view from the library or organization's side, but don't be afraid to delve deeper into the actual policies and procedures.

It is also important to understand what the function of the human resources office or department is in within an organization. While they do care about individual employees and may advocate on your behalf in certain circumstances, their loyalty and responsibilities are to management. If they seem unusually rigid and rule bound, it is often because they are the organization's first line of defense against legal action. Sometimes they can bend the rules, but other times they simply cannot. Recognizing those limitations is useful. A little HR knowledge can be a powerful tool.

GIVE CHANGE A CHANCE

Speaking of human resources, nothing will put the HR office to the test like organizational change. Libraries and cultural heritage institutions in particular are often accused of being too slow to adapt. Sometimes our efforts to change are thwarted by outside forces, but it is often our own resistance that holds us back. Change that is seemingly benign is often met with resistance, so it's not surprising that significant organizational change is likely to encounter full-on opposition, confrontation, and sabotage. If you demonstrate a willingness to not only roll with the changes, but to embrace them and facilitate them where you can, you will earn the undying gratitude of those above you.

It seems somewhat trite to say that library and information organizations are grappling with unprecedented change, but it is as true now as it has ever been. Certainly, the pace of innovation shows no signs of slowing and there is no question that it has an impact on the work we do. Nevertheless, the ability to recognize when change is needed—whether it involves a process, a service, or a way in which people or things are organized—is part of a critical skill set.

As a subject specialist, we are trained to keep a close eye on the trends in topics and research methods impacting our fields. We stay on top of current best practices in instruction, assessment, and collection development. Look for ways to change the way you do your job for the better—whether it is more effective instruction, using data to make decisions about collections, or introducing a process to enhance services—and be creative. Then apply those same skills to other areas of the organization and the larger information environment. Learn about the broader trends impacting the profession and educate yourself on possible disruptive technologies. How will the OA movement alter the way we collect, make accessible, and archive the scholarly record? How can the new information literacy standards be implemented at your institution to have a meaningful impact? Can the library partner with faculty to develop an open textbook that will help the institution deal with the cost of a college education? How can the library develop apps that will serve the broader community of scholars? Disruptive as it might be, change is constant and your capacity to adapt and lead change will prepare you to move up in an ever-changing information environment.

LEAD

I have peppered this chapter with several nods to taking advantage of opportunities to demonstrate leadership qualities. Now I am going to be explicit: LEAD. Before you fall into the trap of believing that the only way to get leadership experience is to be in a position of authority, let me dispel that myth. You do not need authority to lead. Our organizations are littered with supervisors, managers, and people in positions of authority who are not leaders. Another common mistake is to assume that just because you are very good at being a subject specialist, that you are a born leader. Leadership involves a set of skills, some of which will come naturally to you and others you can develop through training, observation, and experience.

One of the most important skills or characteristics a leader has is empathy—the ability to understand the position of others. As I mentioned earlier, working collaboratively, as part of a team, task force, or committee, is one of the best places to begin to hone this skill. Becoming in tune with what motivates or inhibits your colleagues starts with paying attention to the subtleties of a person's actions, getting to know something about them, and acknowledging their perspective. You don't have to be everyone's best friend, but gaining insight into what makes the people you work with tick and connecting to people on a personal level will help build their trust and make them more likely to follow your lead.

Another misperception of leadership is that it somehow requires you to be aggressive, pushy, or confrontational. While there is nothing wrong with being assertive or confident in your views and ideas, like most people, librarians and information professionals tend not to react positively to the "in your face" approach to anything ... ever. Remember that your colleagues are a sharp bunch, so you need to present your ideas clearly and concisely. If you are trying to persuade your team to take a new approach or introduce a new service or resource, approach it as you would an instruction session—know your subject so well that you could explain it to a first-year English student. We also know from instruction that a one-shot session is not where it ends. It takes time for ideas to sink in and for all the questions to be addressed. You can be persistent without being annoying. Some things take time to catch on. If you have data to back up your plan or idea, or the topic lends itself to a more graphic explanation, use images or videos to get your point across.

Along those lines, leaders make things happen; they innovate; they create. As a subject specialist you have a fair amount of autonomy to initiate new services or procedures to enhance your ability or make what you do more effective.

Even if it is not accepted on a broader scale, introducing something new and following it through to implementation is a valuable skill. Along the way, you may need to contend with bureaucratic obstacles or organizational politics, but use those impediments or complications as problems to be solved rather than barriers to success. If something you try fails, that's OK, too. Just dust yourself off and try again. Perseverance and problem solving are critical leadership skills that will serve you well when it is time to move up. Finally, if you are interested in moving up and taking on a leadership position, look for professional development opportunities to learn more about the topic. There is no shortage of leadership institutes, workshops, and seminars out there, including the American Library Association Leadership Institute, the Association of College and Research Libraries/Harvard Advanced Leadership Institute for Senior Academic Librarians, the UCLA Senior Fellows Program, the Northern Exposure to Leadership Institute, and the Leading Change Institute, just to name a few. In addition to being exposed to key leadership skills and principles, these gatherings offer something you can't get reading a book, watching a TED Talk, or following a blog. They give you access to a close network of colleagues that can be invaluable to you throughout your career.

FINAL WORDS

The ability to develop subject expertise has always been and will continue to be a critical element of our work as librarians and information professionals. Regardless of the type of library, archive, or cultural heritage institution you work in, the public—our users—rely on our expertise. It is often our innate curiosity, that insatiable desire to find the answer and to learn more that drew us to this profession and continues to keep us excited and engaged. Our willingness to apply ourselves to expand our knowledge, develop a new skill set, and advance our understanding is an important characteristic and a key factor in preparing for the next step in your career. Putting the same effort into refining those more intangible social and emotional skills that enable us to question what we do, adapt to change, and make things happen is also critical to your success. Finally, find a mentor (or several mentors)—someone you can trust and turn to when you are not sure how to handle a situation, when you need advice, or when you just need to vent. Ideally, make it someone you respect and can learn from, but also recognize that they are not perfect. If the person is genuine, they will share their mistakes and let you learn along with them. I was drawn to this profession because of the smart, generous, and caring people who inhabit our organizations and they have never disappointed. Regardless of the path you take, value your colleagues along the way and make your career one of meaning. As you begin your own professional journey, mapping out the trajectory of your own career—preparing yourself to move up the ladder—I encourage you to be open, curious, and reflective.

INDEX

American Geological Institute, 19
American Historical Association, 116
The American Historical Review, 116
American Indian Library Association, 84
American Institute of Physics, 19
American Libraries, 10, 116
American Library Association (ALA), 8,
26, 28, 60, 64, 74, 81, 84; "Academic
Interview Process," 145; accredited
degree program, 100; accredited library
schools, 135; Library Instruction Round
Table (LIRT), 8–9; online course and
webinar offerings of, 113; Reference and
User Services Association, 121–22;
Science and Technology Section, 19;
Spectrum Scholarships, 135; teacher
education, 105
American Library Association Leadership
Institute, 166
American Literature, 75
American Mathematical Society, 20
American Medical Informatics
Association, 137
American Philosophical Association, 116
American Physical Society, 20
American Psychological Association
(APA), 96, 99
American Society for Engineering
Education, 36; Engineering Libraries
Division, 36–37
American Statistical Association, 20
American Theological Library
Association, 111, 116
Arbeitsgemeinschaft fur juristisches
Bibliotheks- und
Dokumentationswesen, 65
Archival Outlook, 116
area studies librarianship: career paths,
81–82; internships, 80–81;
intersections with other disciplines,
78; introduction, 77; master of library
science and other coursework, 80;
professional organizations, 82–84;
publications to follow, 84–85; special
requirements for the position, 79–80;
work experience, 80–81; workplaces,
78–79
ARLIS New and Emerging Professionals
group (ARLISNAP), 47

Art Bulletin, 47
Art Documentation, 47
Artforum, 47
Art in America, 47
Art Institute of Chicago, 40, 46
Art Journal, 47
art librarianship: career paths, 46;
internships, 45–46; intersections with
other disciplines, 42–43; introduction,
39–42; master of library science and
other coursework, 44–45; professional
organizations, 46–47; publications to
follow, 47; special requirements for the
position, 44; work experience, 45–46;
workplaces, 43–44
Art Libraries Society of North America
(ARLIS/NA), 47
Art Museum Libraries and Librarianship
(Benedetti), 41
Artnews, 47
The Art Newspaper, 47
arXiv, 32
arXiv.org, 16
Asian African and Middle Eastern
Section (AAMES), 116
Asian American Librarians Caucus
(AALC), 84
Asian Art Museum, San Francisco, 43–44
Asian Pacific American Librarians
Association (APALA), 84
Asian studies, 83–84
Assessment Tool for Sociology
Collections and Services, 104
Association for Asian Studies, 83
Association for Information Science and
Technology (ASIS&T), 137;
Scientific and Technical Information
Special Interest Group, 36–37
Association for Library Collections &
Technical Services (ALCTS), 137
Association of Academic Health Sciences
Libraries, 136
Association of Architecture School
Librarians, 47
Association of College and Research
Libraries (ACRL), 8, 18, 28, 36–37,
54–55, 64, 135, 166; *ACRL
Environmental Scan*, 122; Asian,
African, and Middle Eastern Section

ABOUT THE EDITOR AND CONTRIBUTORS

THE EDITOR

KAREN SOBEL is a Research & Instruction Librarian and Associate Professor at the University of Colorado Denver, where she performs instruction, research assistance, and collection development. In 2012, she wrote the well-received *Information Basics for College Students* with Libraries Unlimited. Karen is deeply committed to helping new academic librarians find fulfilling work.

THE CONTRIBUTORS

JENNIFER ALLISON is a Librarian for Foreign, Comparative, and International Law at the Harvard Law School Library. In addition to her responsibilities as a reference librarian, she specializes in research support and collection development for German-language jurisdictions. She earned her BA (English and German) from Pacific Lutheran University, after which she taught English in Germany as a Fulbright award recipient. She then worked for several years as a technical writer in the software industry. Following that, she earned a JD from the Pepperdine University School of Law and an MLIS from San Jose State University. She serves on the Editorial Board of the *Foreign Law Guide*, a major research and reference source for foreign legal materials published by Brill, for which she is also the editor of the content for Austria and Germany. She is also a contributing author to Brill's *Sources of State Practice in International Law*.

STEPHANIE BONJACK is the Head of the Howard B. Waltz Music Library at the University of Colorado Boulder. She holds a Bachelor of Music in Vocal Performance from Butler University, a Master of Library and Information Science from Dominican University, and a Master of Music in Musicology from Northwestern University. Prior to her position at CU Boulder, she served as the Head of the Music Library at the University of Southern California. She is an active member of the Music Library Association, having recently served as Fiscal Officer for the organization. She is a regular reviewer of books on popular music for *Music Reference Services Quarterly*. Her research interests focus on the role of technology in the lives of musicians and the challenges music libraries face in staying relevant in the digital age.

JASON COLEMAN is an Undergraduate and Community Services Librarian at Kansas State University Libraries. He coordinates K-State Libraries' Ask A Librarian Team and supervises three members of Hale Library's Reference Team. Jason earned an MLS from Emporia State University in 2007. He has published three previous articles/chapters related to the work of reference and instruction generalists.

JOSIAH M. DREWRY is the Librarian for Business, Economics, and Sociology at the University of North Carolina at Chapel Hill (UNC). He is a research partner and instructor for students and faculty in these departments, and coteaches a graduate course on research in business and economics at UNC's School of Information and Library Science. Josiah also consults with students and faculty in UNC's Minor in Entrepreneurship, as well as individual entrepreneurs, start-ups, small businesses, and other public, private, and nonprofit organizations across the state. Josiah holds an MBA from North Carolina State University, and an MSLS from the University of North Carolina at Chapel Hill.

LISE M. DYCKMAN is a former Senior Acquisitions Editor with Libraries Unlimited; for decades she worked in academic and special libraries, most recently as the Library Director for the California Institute of Integral Studies. Prior to that position, she was Director of Library and AV Services for St. Mary's Medical Center, which at the time had one of the last remaining inpatient psychiatric units in a teaching hospital in the city of San Francisco. She is still an active member of the Northern California Consortium of Psychology Libraries, and has held committee roles with RUSA, ACRL, and NCNMLG. She has an MLIS degree from Drexel University, and an MA in American Civilization/Museum Curatorship from the University of Pennsylvania.

ARIANNE HARTSELL-GUNDY is the Head of the Humanities Section and Librarian for Literature and Theater Studies at Duke University. She was previously the Humanities Librarian at Miami University in Ohio. She holds a Dual Master's in Comparative Literature/Library Science from Indiana University, and a BA in English from the University of Missouri–Columbia. She is the coeditor of *Digital Humanities in the Library: Challenges and Opportunities for Subject Specialists* and the coauthor of *Literary Research and British Postmodernism: Strategies and Sources.*

DIXIE A. JONES holds a Master of Library Science from Louisiana State University, Baton Rouge. She served as President of the Medical Library Association from 2013to 2014. She has also received the Lucy B. Foote Award from the Subject Specialists' Section of the Louisiana Library Association (2014). In addition, Ms. Jones has served as a Distinguished Member of the Academy of Health Information Professionals since 1990.

ZAHRA BEHDADFAR KAMAREI is the Director of Science and Engineering Libraries at the University of Rochester. Prior to this position, she was the Head of Science Libraries at the University of North Carolina at Chapel Hill. In addition to her job duties, Zari spends time thinking about what new services she can bring to science libraries to keep them relevant for the users. Zari is also interested in data management and open access. She has a Bachelor of Science degree in Physics and a Master's degree in Library and Information Science. She was a member of a team that created the VISTA Collaboratory (i.e., visualization lab), which won the University of Rochester's Meliora Award.

LAURA KOLTUTSKY has been a Social Sciences Librarian for 14 years. She currently works at the University of Calgary as an Associate Librarian with liaison responsibilities for Social Work, Sociology, and Psychology. Laura coedited the *Library Juice Press Handbook of Intellectual Freedom: Concepts, Cases, and Theories* in 2014.

SHARI LASTER is the Government Data & Information Librarian at the University of California, Santa Barbara. She is an active member of the Government Documents Round Table of the American Library Association, and a past chair of the Depository Library Council, the advisory body for the Federal Depository Library Program. Her professional interests include government information in the context of information literacy, trends and issues in identifying and capturing the national collection of U.S. government publications, and usability issues. She received her MSLS from the University of North Carolina at Chapel Hill and her BA in philosophy and religious studies from Rice University.

JACK M. MANESS, MLS, is an Associate Professor and Director of the Sciences Department in the University of Colorado Boulder Libraries. He has over 10 years' experience as a science and engineering subject specialist and has published over a dozen scholarly articles. His work is heavily cited and has been translated into many languages. He has chaired committees for ACRL's Science and Technology Section and is a manuscript referee for several important journals in library and information science.

EMILEE MATHEWS has been the Research Librarian for Visual Arts at University of California, Irvine since 2013. Before then, she served as the Interim head of the Fine Arts Library at Indiana University, Bloomington, where she also obtained her two master's degrees, in library science and art history. She is currently engaged in an NEH grant-funded project to pilot linked open data on UCI's collection of artists' books. She also researches and writes on convergences of digital humanities, new media art, and information science.

LISA NORBERG is cofounder and principal of K I N Consultants, Ltd., a nonprofit organization providing strategic and operational guidance to academic and research libraries, scholarly societies, and other mission-driven schools and organizations. She has over 20 years of experience in academic librarianship, having held positions at Barnard College of Columbia University, the University of North Carolina at Chapel Hill, Penn State University at Harrisburg, and George Mason University. She is a visiting faculty member at Pratt Institute's School of Information Science, where she teaches a course on strategic leadership and lectures on topics related to academic libraries. She has been an active member and officeholder in ALA and ACRL and is the recipient of several awards, including the ACRL LPSS Marta Lange/CQ Press Award and the ACRL Instruction Section Innovation Award.

BETSAIDA M. REYES is an Assistant Librarian at the University of Kansas. She is the librarian for Spanish, Portuguese, Latin American, and Caribbean Studies. Reyes has a Master of Science in Information Science and a Master of Arts in Hispanic Literature and Linguistics from the

University at Albany, SUNY. In 2013, she was awarded the Seminar on the Acquisition of Latin American Library Materials (SALALM) Scholarship.

KELLI J. TREI is a Biosciences Librarian and Assistant Professor, University Library at the University of Illinois at Urbana-Champaign. As a Biosciences Librarian she manages the collection, research, and reference services within the life sciences and bioengineering. Her research interests include preparedness of science librarians for the field and increasing scientific information literacy for all users in regards to available resources and critical assessment of information. Kelli worked as a research scientist for Archer Daniels Midland Co. for 14 years before becoming a science librarian.

CHELLA VAIDYANATHAN is the Curator of 19th–21st Century Rare Books and Manuscripts in the Department of Special Collections and Archives at the Sheridan Libraries of Johns Hopkins University. She is also the Academic Liaison Librarian for the Department of History, Department of Anthropology, Center for Africana Studies, Program in Latin American Studies, and Program in Islamic Studies. Her responsibilities include building, managing, and assessing print collections and electronic resources for History, Anthropology, Africana Studies, Latin American Studies, and Islamic Studies. Moreover, she is in charge of developing nineteenth- to twenty-first-century rare books, manuscripts, and ephemera. She loves working with rare books and teaching classes using materials from special collections as well as bibliographic instruction sessions. Chella has taught credit-based intersession classes using print, digital, and special collections materials that offer hands-on research experience in the humanities to undergraduate students. Particularly, she is interested in integrating digital primary source materials and Web 2.0 tools like blogs, wikis, Flickr, YouTube, etc., in her classes. She is also interested in the application of GIS to the discipline of humanities and in digital humanities in general. She holds an MLS from the University of Maryland, College Park, a Master of Arts in Modern European history from Southern Illinois University, Edwardsville (SIUE), and a Master of Philosophy in History, and a Master Arts in South Asian/Indian history from the University of Madras. Chella was a Fellow in the Association of Research Libraries' 2013–14 Leadership and Career Development Program (LCDP) and she also participated in the 2009 ALA Emerging Leaders Program.

DIANE ZABEL is the Benzak Business Librarian and Head of the Schreyer Business Library at Penn State University's University Park campus. In 2015 she was awarded The President's Award for Engagement with Students, a Penn State award that recognizes a faculty member who encourages student learning. Ms. Zabel is a past editor of *Reference & User Services Quarterly*. She currently serves on the editorial board of the *Journal of Business & Finance Librarianship*. Ms. Zabel is the coeditor of *Rethinking Collection Development and Management* (Libraries Unlimited, 2014) and the editor of *Reference Reborn: Breathing New Life into Public Services Librarianship* (Libraries Unlimited, 2011). She is an active member of the American Library Association (ALA). Ms. Zabel served as the elected president of the Reference and User Services Association (one of the divisions of ALA) and as an elected member of the governing body of ALA (ALA Council). In 2011 she was the recipient of the Isadore Gilbert Mudge Award, an ALA award that recognizes distinguished contributions in reference librarianship. She holds a master of urban planning degree (1980) and a master of science in library and information science (1982) from the University of Illinois at Urbana-Champaign.